Returning Sanity to the Classroom

Returning Sanity to the Classroom

Eliminating the Testing Mania

Horace "Rog" Lucido

ROWMAN & LITTLEFIELD
Lanham • Boulder • New York • London

Published by Rowman & Littlefield
A wholly owned subsidiary of The Rowman & Littlefield Publishing Group, Inc.
4501 Forbes Boulevard, Suite 200, Lanham, Maryland 20706
www.rowman.com

Unit A, Whitacre Mews, 26-34 Stannary Street, London SE11 4AB

British Library Cataloguing in Publication Information Available

Library of Congress Cataloging-in-Publication Data

Lucido, Horace, 1945–
Returning sanity to the classroom : eliminating the testing mania / Horace "Rog" B. Lucido.
pages cm.
Includes bibliographical references.
ISBN 978-1-4758-1790-4 (cloth : alk. paper) — ISBN 978-1-4758-1791-1 (pbk. : alk. paper) — ISBN 978-1-4758-1792-8 (electronic) 1. Effective teaching—United States. 2. Classroom environment—United States. 3. Group work in education—United States. 4. Education—Aims and objectives—United States. 5. Educational tests and measurements—United States. I. Title.
LB1025.3.L827 2015
371.102—dc23

2015013040

∞ ™ The paper used in this publication meets the minimum requirements of American National Standard for Information Sciences Permanence of Paper for Printed Library Materials, ANSI/NISO Z39.48-1992.

Printed in the United States of America

This book is dedicated to students and teachers whose lives are constrained under the oppression of high-stakes testing.

I am forever grateful to my wife, Vincie, who has supported my vision for forgiving teaching and learning.
—Rog Lucido

Contents

Foreword

The learning of pedagogy is one of the most interesting intellectual paths a human can take. At first pedagogy is learned at the university and later in classrooms as professional teachers continue to reflect and wonder how they can make learning better. Throughout their careers good teachers wonder how they can connect better with their students, how they can help the students connect better with what they should learn in schools, and about the purpose of schooling.

Americans have a great tradition of innovation, reflection, and professional pedagogy. Our tradition goes back to Horace Mann in the beginning of the early nineteenth century when he advocated that teachers should develop as professionals and stop using corporal punishment. Jane Addams and John Dewey at Hull House in Chicago at the turn of the twentieth century together promoted the democratic ideas of social and interactive processes as vital to pedagogy. Democracy was not just about being represented. More importantly, democracy was also about participation in all that people do. Finally, at the end of the twentieth century, Donald Schon emphasized the importance of reflection for professionals and the idea that we should include our personal stories. It is in the spirit and independent tradition of these great Americans that Rog Lucido writes this book and carries these great traditions.

I met Rog in the early part of No Child Left Behind around 2003 as we, along with Elaine Garan, were saddened and outraged by the emphasis of high-stakes state tests on the curriculum and the top-down deskilling of teachers. At that time, teachers were forced to comply rigidly to the teacher's manual and social interaction was limited as direct instruction predominated. Eventually, we formed the Educators and Parents Against Testing Abuse (EPATA), working with educators to limit the overemphasis of grades and scores as ineffective measures of students and their knowledge. Through the Cesar Chavez Conference of Literacy and Educational Policy at California State University, Fresno, we organized educators to make a change. We brought in speakers that reflected a different perspective on teaching and learning such as Gerald Bracey, Stephen Krashen, Donaldo Macedo, Wayne Au, and Jeffrey Duncan-Andrade.

To a certain extent, we did have an effect on the professional and political lives of teachers and students, but we feel that what currently exists falls far short of what Rog outlines in this book *Returning Sanity to the Classroom: Eliminating the Testing Mania*. While currently the relationship between many teachers and their students can be described as adversarial in nature, Rog suggests that we develop a culture of relationship in which teachers act as coaches advocating for their students.

In part, grades distance teachers and students from the content they are trying to learn and from each other. Students' focus becomes not the fascination with our lives and our world, but rather the percentages and points to receive a good grade. Instead, Rog advocates classrooms and relationships between student and teacher that focus on a mutual interest in the ideas of our world. So rather than reporting that a student got an A in English, the student and teacher might describe love of nature in Walt Whitman or the critical essays of Henry David Thoreau. Or instead of being on chapter 10 of the history book the student might describe the vacillations of a president on the brink of war. So the most important thing students might report to their parents is not the grade they got, the affirming comments of the teacher ("Good job John"), or the chapter they are on, but rather the ideas they are curious about.

The teacher's job then is to be a coach who investigates, asks questions, encourages, and guides students toward greater understanding. Instead of using grades as punitive instruments, the teacher would seek to transform and refocus the student toward the ideas. Transformation and reason become the goal instead of students and teachers and not credentialing with grades.

This book is also very practical in describing ways to help students participate as members of the class in fun and social engagements with the content. Students will have to learn to listen better to the teacher and their classmates. All members of the class will have to pay attention to the nonverbal cues such as body language that may communicate more than words. Role playing can help students actively engage in the curriculum as well as representing a range of perspectives.

One of the aspects I like the most about this book is the fun! As Dewey suggests, Rog illustrates his ideas with stories about his football days and popular movies like *The Karate Kid*.

In the end, this book is about developing a philosophy of teaching that builds on the solid American values of the teacher as a true professional. This professional promotes the democratic principles that we cherish as students and as participants in their future. It builds on the idea that schools should promote excellent social relationships and complex understandings about the world.

Glenn L. DeVoogd, PhD
Professor and Chair of the Department of Literacy, Early, Bilingual, and Special Education
California State University, Fresno

Preface

The impetus to write *Returning Sanity to the Classroom: Eliminating the Testing Mania* came from "Forgiving Learning," the last chapter of my previous work, *Educational Genocide: A Plague on Our Children*. I began that chapter with three questions: So what are we to do? If high-stakes testing and all its attendant baggage were to disappear, how could we assess what students know and are able to do? How are we to modify the way in which our classrooms are structured to fit brain-compatible learning?

I realized that while I addressed the salient points of Forgiving Learning, the chapter did not provide the theoretical and pedagogical details that would make its application feasible to the modern classroom. To that end, each chapter in *Returning Sanity to the Classroom: Eliminating the Testing Mania* is set up as one of Forgiving Learning's integral components. How to meld these concepts and suggested activities into the instructor's educational philosophy is up to each classroom practitioner. This is where individual autonomy and creativity can play a large part in this pedagogy.

To whatever degree possible students should be educated on what the teacher is attempting to do and its benefits to their learning. In like fashion parents/guardians should be informed about what the instructor is doing and why. Keep in mind that K–12 educators are an extension of each student's prime teacher(s): their parent(s)/guardian(s). Garnering their support will provide the opportunity for Forgiving Learning to be sustained within each student's family's daily life.

If done properly, Forgiving Learning can become the central theme of schools, districts, and communities. If this were to come to pass, it would not have to be "re-taught" at each grade level but reinforced, modified, and/or adjusted to fit new and different teachers and classrooms. When one mentions ice cream to another person they have the general idea of what it means, but one is also aware that it comes in different flavors and textures. Likewise with Forgiving Learning: it will hopefully become that familiar and one only has to look at what "flavor" it is in this new time and place.

Acknowledgments

It is more than likely that I would have never come to the concept of Forgiving Learning without my high school football coach, Cal Hilgenburg, forgiving my previous poor play then asking me to be a starter in the most important game of our season. I am so grateful for my children, Adri, Joe, Vince, Simon, and Tim who, as they grew, modeled for me what persistence and learning from their mistakes really means. I continue to thank all of those educators, parents, and community members who have formed the foundation of Educators and Parents Against Testing Abuse (EPATA). Across the United States is the work of the national Assessment Reform Network (ARN), especially Monty Neil and Bob Schaefer. Susan Ohanian, Steven Krashen, Jim Horn, and Marion Brady lead the fight against high-stakes testing. California State University Kremen School of Education continues to be on the cutting edge of teacher development, especially Dr. Glenn DeVoogt, who was kind enough to write the foreword to this book. While in these groups and among these individuals I have been the most nurtured and have shared and enhanced my dreams for education.

I am so thankful for the following educators who not only provided the persistent vision of what should be in our schools, but were also willing reviewers of the original draft of this book: Helen Pitton, Linda Caffejian, Dr. Glenn DeVoogt, and Marion Brady. A special thank you to Gordon Wiens, who was also a reviewer, and began his teaching as one of my student teachers and continued to team teach with me using Forgiving Learning for many years. Their work continues to give me hope for a better future for students.

It goes without saying that I am indebted to publishers Rowman and Littlefield, who saw value in this book through Dr. Thomas F. Koerner, the vice president and publisher. I am grateful for all the help Christine Fahey, assistant editor for education, provided with much of the detail work.

How can I ever repay my wife, Vincie, for her ongoing reading and commentary; but more so, for her daily sacrifices of time and energy to keep me focused by continually reminding me of the importance of this work? And finally for my son, Joseph, a current fifth-grade teacher, who is not only living in the current high-stakes testing atmosphere, but is willing to take a risk by making his values known through his writings and activism.

I am humbled by the selflessness of all of the aforementioned in helping to make this book possible. It surely is a tribute to the hope contained within the human spirit.

Introduction

REFORM?

It seems like education is on a never-ending quest to be "reformed." The current trend began with the successful USSR orbiting of Sputnik on October 4, 1957, and reached a crescendo in 1983 with the publication of "A Nation at Risk." This flawed report spoke of a "rising level of mediocrity" in our schools when in fact the evidence it cited was greatly skewed toward that desired outcome (http://www.edutopia.org/landmark-education-report-nation-risk).

FALSE CONCLUSION

Engendering public fear, the message continues today: "American students are behind those of many countries. Our dominance of military and economic strength is on the decline. We are losing our competitiveness." The root cause of this false conclusion was laid at the feet of our schools by the U.S. corporate world. But when viewed from an international perspective our perceived "plight" was due in fact not to schools but to American social, business, and political failings.

NO CORRELATION

The World Economic Forum researchers have concluded that the U.S. economic competitiveness has weaknesses. The report reads that the "weaknesses include the business communities' criticism of the public and private institutions, that there is a great lack of trust in politicians, and a lack of a strong relationship between government and business. And the U.S. debt continues to grow."

THE RELATIONSHIP IS MOOT

According to the World Economic Forum, student test scores on international tests in reading, mathematics, and science were not even mentioned as connected to the weakening of the United States's ability to compete. The relationship is moot. (World Economic Forum Report 2011).

CLAIM NOT SUPPORTED

Further, in renowned researcher Christopher H. Tienken's *Rankings of International Achievement Test Performance and Economic Strength: Correlation or Conjecture?* he states: "In the case of the United States, the data does not support the claim that a correlation exists between performance on international tests of mathematics and science and economic strength as measured by the Global Competitive Index." (http://journals.sfu.ca/ijepl/index.php/ijepl/article/view/110/44)

NCLB

With many studies demonstrating that 80 to 90 percent of student achievement is due to factors outside of school, how can we consider changes in our schooling as the solution to our economic problems? Based on the principle that schools were the culprit, over the last fourteen years Congress and the 2001 administration charged ahead with a "plan" that was thought to fix all of this: No Child Left Behind (NCLB).

THE PLAN

The plan's fundamental paradigm was for each state to create a set of educational standards, ask educators to teach to those standards, test students on those standards, report their results back to the U.S. Department of Education, and determine if each state is progressing at a predetermined rate that would culminate in 2014 with all students being proficient in mathematics and English language arts.

HIGH-STAKES TESTING CULTURE

This "plan" was the genesis of today's high-stakes testing culture. They are called high-stakes tests because the scores are then used to judge students, teachers, schools, districts, and states. These scores are not a valid way to make educational decisions. (See *Educational Genocide: A Plague on our Children* at http://www.worldcat.org/title/educational-genocide-a-plague-on-our-children/oclc/606051706).

SANCTIONS

If schools did not make adequate yearly progress (AYP) on student proficiency percentages, they were met with varying degrees of sanctions. Districts, schools, and teachers came under more and more restrictive and proscriptive mandates or their schools were reconstituted with new administrators and teachers with state "take-over" as the ultimate punishment.

NEVER TESTED

The 2001 No Child Left Behind Act (NCLB) was never tested for its effectiveness before enactment. The results are now evident: *academic stagnation*. It did not work! Former U.S. assistant secretary of education Diane Ravitch writes:

> Because of NCLB, more than 80 percent of our nation's public schools will be labeled "failures" this year. By 2014, on the NCLB timetable of destruction, close to 100 percent of public schools will have "failed" in their efforts to reach the unreachable goal of 100 percent proficiency in reading and math. Has there ever been a national legislative body anywhere else in the world that has passed legislation that labeled almost every one of its schools a failure? [1]

REVIVAL?

Recent attempts at NCLB revival include both waivers directed at states and districts who are trying to escape the law's harsh sanctions as well as stimulation with the "Race to the Top" funding program. Both attempts are hinged on states accepting a set of national education standards called the "Common Core Standards" along with national testing to follow. This new "plan" was never piloted and has no evidence of success, once again making millions of U.S. students guinea pigs. Essentially it says to the states, "Accept these standards or else you will not qualify for these funding programs."

WRONG QUESTIONS

The problem with all of these "reform" efforts is that they ask the wrong questions from the wrong perspectives. They start from the outside—national and state initiatives—with the hope of improving individual student learning within the confines of the classroom. How threats and coercion from the highest levels of government could possibly translate into students becoming more eager and desirous to learn in the classroom is almost farcical. These "reform" efforts were not initiated by practitioners who work daily with students. None of these programs began by asking cadres of teachers: "What are the classroom practices that best engage students in learning?"

IMPROVEMENT

Improvement is what this book is all about. As educationally engaged professionals, parents, and community members, we should have as part of our ongoing interest the improvement of the learning atmosphere for our students. This interest is not in reaction to economic fearmongering but is a genuine human response to benefit our youth. I suggest a restructuring that begins in the classroom that then moves outward to schools, districts, and states as a means of supporting individual student learning.

EXPERIENCES

What I share here is my personal experience of having integrated various concepts and strategies that I have found to be most beneficial to my students. While many of these ideas may have been used in isolation from each other, I have put them together into a cogent practical and successful pedagogy. I call it "Forgiving Learning."

THE BRAIN

The human brain is the organ for learning, whether inside or outside of school. Each of our bodily organs has a particular function within the context of living. As educators we hope that all of our students' organs are working well to the benefit of their health and well-being. But in particular we focus on the brain because one of its primary functions is not only a clearing house for what enters through the senses, but also a seeker of patterns and connections.

CONDITIONS

The brain learns from all the random inputs that daily life puts before each of us. I address the question of what the conditions are under which the brain operates with highest efficiency. Which of those conditions is the classroom practitioner responsible for maximizing? Which of those conditions is the school, family life, and the greater community responsible for providing? What aspects of having a healthy brain is the student responsible for?

NATURAL LEARNING

The human brain makes decisions. Each of us has a preferred way of making them. These preferences can be both a strength and a weakness. The teacher needs to know and understand how these preferences influence the student's response to the various strategies that are employed in the classroom. They also need to have a working knowledge of their own teaching preferences and how that can impact student engagement.

PREWIRED

The all-encompassing idea is that over the millennia the human species has interacted with its environment and evolved a process of natural learning. Our brains come to us prewired and ready to follow its programming of learning from its mistakes while making positive changes along the way to success. The heart fulfills its purpose in circulating the blood. All the other organs follow suit in performing their natural functions. Just like any of the other bodily organs, the neocortex portion of the brain seeks to fulfill its major role: it wants to learn.

ADAPTABLE

Forgiving Learning is therefore a pedagogy of educational cooperation. It is one solution to the question of how to create and operate a student-brain-friendly learning atmosphere K–12 and beyond. Forgiving Learning employs strategies that students readily recognize as satisfying their need to know and successfully comprehend the world in which they live. It is presented in a way that is adaptable to multiple teaching styles and of such a nature that it can be modified to best fit classroom modalities that schools and districts have already mandated. Although the principles of Forgiving Learning were developed within high school physics classes, its central tenet of students learning from their mistakes with multiple opportunities without penalty can be applied to any grade level or course offering. Errors can be redeemed.

EDUCATION FROM LIVING

Learning from failure is not just the method in which a baby learns to walk, but over the millennia has become a most viable learning process for all human beings. The core elements of Forgiving Learning will be recognized by all adults who support students' healthy development and can also be of great benefit to the community at large. I long to see what Edgar Z. Freedenberg so perceptibly envisioned:

Then, there may come a time when you can't even tell education from living.[2]

NOTES

1. Diane Ravitch, "NCLB: End It, Don't Mend It," *Education Week*, http://blogs.edweek.org/edweek/Bridging-Differences/2011/10/dear_deborah_have_you_been.html, accessed October 25, 2011.

2. Beatrice Gross and Ronald Gross, *Radical School Reform* (New York: Simon and Schuster, 1970).

ONE

The Beginnings—Does This Count?

It was 1982 and I had been teaching physics in a private Catholic high school for fifteen years. There was a dream, a belief that students who took physics really wanted to learn it and that physics teaching, in some unique way, was going to be of service in their desire to know the world through different eyes. That year was a wakeup call. Not that there were inklings of this before, but this year it just leaped out: this wasn't teaching "physics" but it was teaching a physics *course*.

DISAPPOINTMENT

A sinking heart would result when finding students plagiarizing their lab reports and problem sets. Elation would follow when completing reading through an assignment in which there was convincing evidence that the work had been done individually and honestly. Disappointment would again rise to the surface when students did poorly on a test, then rushed to set up a time for a make-up test so teacher and students could feel better about it. But sometimes I cringed whenever a student would come to ask why he got a nine and not a ten on his lab report.

WRONG QUESTION

With the closing of the grading period came the rush to the front desk: "How many points do I have, Mr. Lucido?," "Can I do any extra credit points, Mr. Lucido?," "What do I gotta do to get an A?," "What can I do to raise my grade, Mr. L.?" Then came the sob stories of how grades will make or break their grade point averages, guarantee entrance into college, lower insurance rates, earn the car mom and dad have been promising, or mean freedom to be off "restriction." But without a doubt the straw that broke this teacher's back was the question that found its form in so many variations but always the same empty meaning: "Does this assignment count?"

NO GRADES?

It was with this question and its implications ringing all around that the realization rose to the surface that these kids didn't want to learn physics, they just wanted a good grade. To most of them learning was an unnecessary luxury. It was then that sly thoughts came to mind: "What if they didn't have grades? Boy that would get 'em." But then the sobering thought: "Would it get this teacher? Could physics teaching actually take place without the whip of grades; would the students listen? Would teaching the love of physics be exciting enough for this grade-conscious group?"

OBSERVANT

As if all of this wasn't enough, self-observation of the time and energy spent as a teacher became clearly evident. Too much time was spent deciding whether a particular problem deserved a six or a seven, whether a "C" was 68 percent or 71 percent, or whether 341 semester points warranted a "D" or "D+," adding up the total points accrued in a grading period or semester, then announcing the point spread for "As," "Bs," "Cs," "Ds," and the "F"!

BARRIER

Frequently, a student would have earned so many extra points to make up for his "B" that his total points would now fall into the "A" category. Reluctantly, the recorded grade would be an "A" but both of us knew that there was something wrong here. Points and grades were definitely becoming a barrier between teacher and students. Many ingenious methods were tried to break down this obstacle. For example, making extra credit only a certain percent of the grade with an elaborate calculation system was attempted.

KEEPING COUNT

But it all came down to the same thing: the students and their teacher were both keeping count! Just like their teacher, students were using numbers and letters as a "scientific" justification for their grades. While spending as much time dealing with grades as actually teaching physics and helping students, there was an "aha" moment of enlightenment. Arriving at a letter or score was not as perfect as was assumed.

NOT OBJECTIVE

While reflecting on this personal attitude toward grades, the realization became clear that this physics teacher was operating on the underlying assumption that he actually was being objective. Like a pan balance or a meter stick, was he capable of making quantitative measurements, determining the values of labs, problems, and quizzes with minimal uncertainty? Of course he did not have that ability. He had often graded papers in the morning, when he was awake and alert, in a significantly different way than when at home late in the evening or in the psychological "nap" time of his afternoons! Realizing this, it was not surprising to read in Francis Evans's article,

> Approximately 100 teachers were asked to mark a paper on a scale of 100 points, with 75 points being a passing mark. In English, a range of 39 points was found. Critics argued that since English is a subjective area of study, the findings were not surprising, but they were astonished when a similar variability—a range of about 45 points was found in geometry. These studies were landmarks in casting doubt on the reliability of testing and grading procedures as they demonstrated that the variability in marks was not a function of the subject area, but appeared to be a function of the grader. A later study by Bells demonstrated that teachers, when requested to re-grade a series of geography and history examinations did so with low reliability. Tieg reported that a single teacher, given the same test papers to rescore after a two-month interval, assigned marks that differed on the average (on a 100-point scale) from the marks first assigned. Bracht found that the first and second scores given to a single, brief essay question correlated 0.50 when reread by the same instructor , and .47 when read by a different instructor.[1]

This reading reinforced the painfully acquired awareness that numerical or letter grading is an attempt to measure the immeasurable. Certainly one of the qualities of a good scientist is to be cognizant of the kinds of things that can and can't be measured.

PERSON TO PERSON

Mulling over this, the awareness came: "What should teachers want to say to their students when they answer a question well or incorrectly, or perhaps come to a conclusion that is not warranted by their laboratory data?" Perhaps the instructor really wants to say, "Frank, that's good so far but you need to work harder at understanding vector concepts." "Mary, please look at your uncertainties again and re-evaluate." "Paul, this is fantastic; keep it up." Then why not just say that?

SPEAK

Say what really needs to be said. Speak to students as they deserve: one person to another, as teacher to student, as one who is concerned that Frank and Mary overcome their weaknesses and that Paul feels encouraged at his understanding. Grades had been clouding the issue and the issue was physics. By attempting to quantify their work this process was actually feeding their grade-conscious syndrome.

SCHOOL POLICY

Although there was a school policy that required letter grades (and in some cases Pass/Fail) at semester end, it was decided that for the love of self, students, and physics a process would be initiated to develop an evaluation system that would help remove grade consciousness and encourage content consciousness. The major elements of the evolving evaluation system rested on these foundations:

1. The system should encourage students to focus on the physics of the real world around them for their own sake and not for grades.
2. The system should enable teachers to spend more personal time in written and oral contact with their students.
3. Quantitative evaluations should be given only weekly, and then only if requested by the student or required by the administration.

PARENTAL EXPECTATIONS

At the beginning of the course, a two-page form was sent home whose primary purpose was to clarify for the students their reasons for taking physics and their expectations of the course. Students were often either following the crowd or were somehow convinced that physics was a college requirement. Then, too, many came to the class with expectations that were rarely brought to their conscious minds. Thus, in order to clarify their intentions, the form asked them to write about their expectations of the course.

PARENTS

The second reason the form was sent home was to help the students learn why their parents wanted them to take physics. Parents had success expectations for their children that many times they would only express in terms of specific grades. The third major goal of this introductory "assignment" was to let the students know that their instructor took the teaching of physics seriously and also took them seriously.

FROM GRADES TO PHYSICS

The students were then told that all of their problem sets, lab reports, quizzes, and the final exam would be evaluated with written comments on their papers and would also contain a summary comment written directly to them. The attempt at this time was to communicate the desire and hope that they can shift their focus from concern about grades to concern about physics. It did take a little more time to read and write comments. But when considering the time to add points, record those points and grades, sometimes make a curve and average the scores at grading time, it was much more energizing to write comments for their evaluations.

SHOCK

For most students, the revelation that they were in physics to enjoy and learn physics (and that the grade is secondary) was a shock. Most of their other courses had moved from topic to topic, chapter to chapter, each unit moderated by a graded quiz and closed with a scored test. It became obvious that many students had been conditioned to believe that this was the only pattern for education. One of their first questions was "Without a grade or a score how will I know how I'm doing?"

BLIND

It was inquired of them if they could ever imagine hearing that question being asked by an athlete out for a sport for the first time. It's assumed that the coach will tell them when they had or had not acquired the appropriate skills. It was clear that grades had so removed the evaluation process from the innate internal senses of the students that they were blind to their own progress unless an external "quantifier" informed them.

COMMENTS

While it was important that their progress be continually commented upon for better or worse, the comment should take on a form that called for students to assess their own work. A number or letter would have *quantified* their work and brought it to closure. They would have gotten the idea that all the learning was over; no need to even look at the concepts again. Therefore, all student work was first evaluated with comments and returned to them to take home for parent perusal. It was then deposited in a folder filed for later reference. Before beginning this process, sometimes there were written comments like, "This is good, Jack" on papers that had also been graded with a letter grade.

SURVEY

A survey of the students was taken to find out what their interpretation of the comments included with the letter grade were. What was surprisingly discovered was that the students had read these comments as a reflection on the *grade* rather than on their understanding of the physics—as if what was written said, "Receiving this B is good, Jack." Eliminating the grade and having only the comments stimulated students' questions. These questions left the topic at hand open, related it with other material, deepened the teacher-student relationship, and fostered enthusiasm for the study of physics.

CONTENT CONSCIOUSNESS

The vast majority of students soon got into the stream of content consciousness. Each student was met with formally on a quarterly basis. We sat down for ten to fifteen minutes and went through the student's file together. Each of us had the opportunity to share their perceptions of the student's strengths and weaknesses. If they wanted a grade, they were asked to first evaluate their own work with a grade and then their teacher followed likewise. Except those students who opted for a Pass/Fail, all were required to have a semester grade, but not a quarter grade. About half of the students wanted grades at quarter time. In the vast majority of cases our letter evaluations were nearly identical. So because of school policy we only had to deal with grades twice a semester at most!

QUALITY TIME

Again, when balancing the quality of this time against the brevity of an impersonal assignment of a grade, the time was well spent. Once students accepted the new approach, a strange phenomenon began to unfold. Because there were no places to get a hold on their grades, they were left with no resort but to get a hold on physics. The "course" became more like one of their other non-graded experiences, such as music lessons, athletics, listening to friends, etc.

FALSE GOAL

Physics became more a part of their lives rather than a task to be completed. Numerical and letter grades had made record keeping easier and reporting to an outside community more concise and time efficient. The strange thing was that the same statement could be said about the way slabs of meat were "graded"! It became clearer that students were people, not things; they had a right to be free to enjoy learning without the false goal of grades to distract them.

RESULTS

What results of this change encouraged its continuation? For starters was the following comment from our vice principal for studies who also taught a class with these physics students in trigonometry: "What are you doing in that class? All I hear in my trig class is physics!" Furthermore, the number of students in the physics classes grew from 50 in 1978–1979, to 60 in 1979–1980, to 120 in 1982–1983 (this out of a student body of 1,500). The word got around that something engaging was happening in the physics class. In the class itself, the excitement could be seen in the students' eyes; there were questions posed for the satisfaction of learning about this or that physics principle, not in anticipation of a test or quiz.

STUDENT RESPONSE

Students spoke of how they discussed physics at their home dinner table, how they were more observant of simple occurrences around them, or how conscious they became of a new view of their common chores. Others jokingly told how it made great conversation on their last date. Both parents and administration were very supportive of all that was going on with this new method in the physics class. At parent-teacher nights continued encouragement was received from parents who really wanted their children to be excited and positive about learning.

GENUINE LEARNING

Under this new evaluation system it was found that the classes as a whole had significantly better understanding and enjoyment of basic physics. One key element here is what is called "genuine" learning. In the past many students had developed the skill of being "smart for a day," the day of the test, after which the knowledge learned was quickly dumped. In discussing this with students it was found that their level of retention demonstrated more genuine learning than "test day" learning.

DISCONNECT

There was an awareness of the apparent disconnect between the verbal/written evaluations during the process of the course and the letter grade that was submitted at semester's end. However, the significant increase in the students' creativity, interest, and understanding coupled with the newfound freedom to be this new kind of teacher provided the encouragement to continue to develop what had been created.

REAL-LIFE EXPERIENCE

The process of this new classroom experience was much closer to the ways students had learned to enjoy a sport, hobby, or some other sought-after skill. This became much more of a real-life experience than a typical school experience. The question, "Does this assignment count?" no longer had relevance because there was no counting. All activities were directed to enhancing students' understanding of physics concepts, not grading them. This process was not seen as a closed one, but just a beginning.

REFLECTION

As the 1982 school year came to an end, there was a reflection on what had been started and then where to go from there. Yes, students' focus began to change from grade consciousness to content consciousness, but there was still a strangely incomplete satisfaction in establishing a classroom pedagogy that was personally fulfilling. Many teachers dream of what they would like their teaching experience to be. They may have had one or more past instructors who embodied important characteristics that they wanted to emulate. Initially working backward here, the process began with examining students to find what characteristics they had when coming into the classroom, then how that could help form this new teaching methodology.

THE FOUR FEARS

The next few years included reflecting on what was observed of students' behaviors and looking for some common traits. As the school year began it could be seen how fearful some students were of their teacher, but also of their fellow students, the physics course they were taking, and then finally of their possible report card grade. These student worries were obvious and for some of the students these fears could be mentally paralyzing. How could physics even begin to be taught if students had hardly walked in the door when these anxieties became operational, essentially blocking their focus on physics because they were exercising their natural instinct to protect themselves from their teacher, fellow students, physics, and their grade?

FEAR OF THE TEACHER

It had taken years of schooling for students to develop these traumas. While knowing it would be impossible to totally eliminate them, a decision was made to develop a method of significantly reducing these classroom fears. Initially, it was not known how to create within students the belief that this course was going to be a successful experience because their instructor was going to be on their side.

ADVERSARIES

Most of these students saw this physics teacher and their other teachers as *adversaries* in their daily school life. It was as if they had to get *through* their teachers each day. How we related to each other was going to determine, in large measure, whether they would have a hopeful or despairing outlook on the whole school year in their physics class.

SERENDIPITY

Then, while having a most serendipitous moment, this question came to mind: "Reviewing the personal schooling of years gone by, who demonstrated the most hope in the upcoming academic year?" It came in a flash: past athletic coaches, of course! From the outset, the clear message was that they were rooting for their athletes. No one knew of an athletic coach who would speak to their team at the beginning of their sporting season and say, "I want some of you to be excellent, some of you good, some average, some poor, and some of you to fail and drop out."

SUCCESS

The desire of coaches of past memory was the success of each and every athlete in their charge. They wanted *everyone* to be excellent. We all knew they were going to make us work hard, but we all had the sense to know that it was going to be for our good, the good of the team, and the pride of the school.

COACHING

It was a given that our former coaches were on our side. And when reflecting on five years as a track coach, without being conscious of it at the time, all fellow coaches exhibited that same mentality. There arose this desire to translate this model into the physics classroom and see what happened. These former coaches seemed to have a way of doing things that were significantly different than what classroom teachers had with their students. They had relationships with their athletes that were not adversarial. The coach was respected as the master of his/her craft with the goal of forming one team with his/her athletes. Camaraderie was not hoped for, it was expected and necessary.

RESEARCH

It started by doing some research into the word "coach." Surprisingly, it was discovered that the word originated from a small village in Hungary called Kocs. This village became quite famous in the 1450s for building "Cinderella" type carriages. These carriages were soon called "coche" (Fr.) because they came from Kocs. (The Hungarian pronunciation sounds like "coach" in English.) As medieval universities began to develop, its instructors were sometimes called "coaches" (Eng.) by their students since they "carried them along" in the fashion of a carriage.

CARRIED ALONG

Well, well! So coaches were really teachers who carried along their students. To be carried along academically by one's instructor is a fairly personal experience exemplified by the "coach's" nurturing and encouraging behavior. Historically, a later evolving approach to university education were those instructors who, rather than "coaching" their students, stood before their classes and espoused or "professed" what they knew to their students, hence being called professors. It seems that with the birth of the industrial and scientific revolutions beginning in the 1800s, university instructors became more associated with the concept of being a "professor" rather than the original university teachers who "coached" their students.

ATHLETIC COACHING

In the early 1800s the concept of coaching, apparently lacking the sophistication to be worthy of the scientific and industrial approach to schooling, instead took on a very effective and firm root in athletic events. So coaches did for athletics what professors were supposed to do for academics. Now the challenge was how to introduce and actualize this mentality into the physics teaching pedagogy. Creatively, the easiest way to begin was to introduce their physics teacher on the first day of class as their "coach."

COACHING WAS FUN

This was planned to be a big deal and to be fun at the same time. Taking a t-shirt made with the school colors and then having the words "PHYSICS COACH" stenciled on both the front and back was a good start. Putting on a shirt and tie on over this became the first day's dress before school began. While beginning to explain to them where the word "coach" came from, the tie was slowly loosened and removed. Then taking off the dress shirt revealed the t-shirt underneath. As this "dress down" continued, finally a whistle was placed around the neck and a coaching hat on the head. The shocked looks on their faces were priceless.

COACH LUCIDO

At the beginning of the school year when taking roll each student was asked what they preferred to be called, not just the name that appeared on the official classroom list from the office. Perhaps a student's real name was Francis, but he preferred Frank, and so forth. Like them, their physics teacher had a preference: to either be called "Coach" or "Coach Lucido." It was explained that their physics coach wanted to be seen as their mentor, as a person in their corner to support, encourage, and direct their learning. There was a desire for them to perceive their teacher as they would expect to see any good coach: knowledgeable, experienced, enthusiastic, and most importantly, interested in each of them as individuals on a path of lifelong learning.

DIFFERENCE?

This started them thinking: "What is this all about? Is this just a change in name only or will things really be different in here than a regular classroom, and if so, in what ways?" Coaching in its present day usage implies being an advocate for the athlete. It is the athlete and the coach who engage in a mutual endeavor to ensure that the athlete continues to improve in the sport. Athletes assume that their coaches will be on their side and that coaches want them to improve. The bottom line was that these students really needed to believe that I would be on their side.

CHANGE IN APPROACH

In order to begin this process of coaching in the classroom a change was needed in the way the students saw their teacher. Their old mentality had to be shaken and then changed to have them look at their teacher through new eyes. Whether in the classroom or in the hallway, whenever they addressed their physics teacher as "coach" a new and healthy sense of camaraderie was evident. Addressing their physics teacher as "coach" did make inroads into their "fear of the teacher." With this change students were found to be much more vulnerable and willing to share events in their daily lives that might be affecting their connection with learning.

PLAYING FIELD

Their physics coach was now on the same side of the "playing field" as his students. Their coach was now less their adversary. It was now themselves and their coach against the challenges of grasping the physics content. They were no longer alone in their desire to be successful in comprehending physics. Their physics coach was seen as being in their corner, doing what was necessary to help them. So now there was created a model of how to begin to minimize the students' fear of their teacher.

FEAR OF OTHER STUDENTS

What about the anxiety of the role that other students in the class might play in their individual learning process? This secondary fear is often the last to be acknowledged by students. Few want to admit that they are academically fearful of other students, either as individuals or ethnicities. When a student enters the classroom on the first day he or she may think something like, "Mary Sue Williams is in here. There goes my A!" Sometimes girls in math and science classes are afraid of the perceived advantage that boys have. Students of one culture known for their academic prowess are seen as competitors to students in another. How should these intra-student issues be addressed?

NEED A TEAM

The answer was as obvious. Most coaches need to have a team and each student needs to have teammates. What if fellow students could experience each other as teammates in the student's corner, pulling for one another? Then the individual student would no longer be alone among peers in this "understanding physics" task. Now they would have other allies besides their coach: other students as a classroom full of supporters. It was found that this kind of teaming began to alleviate the tensions based on any perceived artificial rivalry.

TEAM BUILDING

As their coach there was a desire for students to enjoy the classroom atmosphere where fear of other students, especially as competitors, could be minimized. Using a teaming structure facilitated students getting to know their teacher and fellow students as helpful companions on this educational journey. Initial and ongoing team building activities outside of subject matter content established relationships of fraternity.

UNDERSTANDING

Classroom exercises and activities utilizing students' learning styles, stereotypes, positive and negative criticism, thoughts vs. feelings, opinions vs. values, the importance of learning from mistakes, and affirming oneself and others set the tone for understanding and mutual respect. (More on this in chapter 4.)

AFFECTIVE PROGRAM

These insights were coupled with methods for enhancing listening skills, such as body language awareness, checking for understanding, and distinguishing hearing from listening. While this entire affective program took place during the first few weeks of school, frequent reminders and related activities were established throughout the school year. This emphasized the importance of healthy human relationships to student learning and primed the students for openness to course content.

NOT DOG-EAT-DOG

Of course it was well known that some classrooms operated on the mentality of personal competition between students. This was obvious in the way grading curves were created, scores were announced or posted, grades and progress histograms were used, and how praise of one or more student's testing successes all were used to encourage students to compete with one another. This competitive mindset supported the philosophy that "it's a dog-eat-dog world" out there so we had better be that way in here. This worldview reinforced the idea that others on this planet, fellow students included, were locked into competition, rather than seeking to cooperate with one another.

COOPERATION

Not wanting to buy into this competition model, the physics course was evolving into a new and different paradigm based on Forgiving Learning. This new structure was to be dependent upon *cooperation* between team members, not competition. Learning how to speak a foreign language, how to write creatively, or calculate the area under a curve was difficult enough without the added anxiety of competing with the person sitting next to you.

EVERYONE

It is clear that on most athletic teams there is competition between team members for a place on the squad. This is because there are predefined numbers allowed on each team. The physics students did not suffer from this limitation since *everyone* could be on the team! We can begin to develop the kind of cooperation and communication that was going to be required when they worked with others within the classroom and outside in the real world.

PROJECT 2061

Because the focus of the team was to help everyone reach his or her academic potential, the added mentorship of the coach meant that each student had a tremendous support system right in the classroom. Fears of the teacher as an adversary and other students as competitors became mitigated by the initial and ongoing activities and resulting enhanced relationships. Learning then became a shared effort on the part of all. In the document Project 2061: Science for all Americans, the American Association for the Advancement of Science made this quite clear:

> Use a team approach. The collaborative nature of scientific and technological work should be strongly reinforced by frequent group activity in the classroom. Scientists and engineers work mostly in groups and less often as isolated investigators. Similarly, students should gain experience sharing responsibility, for learning with each other. In the process of coming to common understandings, students in a group must frequently inform each other about procedures and meanings, argue over findings, and assess how the task is progressing. In the context of team responsibility, feedback and communication become more realistic and of a character very different from the usual individualistic textbook-homework-recitation approach.[2]

FEAR OF COURSE CONTENT: PHYSICS

With an effective plan in place on how to begin to mitigate teacher-student and student-student anxieties, the next concern was to address student fears of the physics course content. Upon entering the physics classroom some students were convinced by hearsay that their academic success was in doubt. Comments by other students, friends, and even parents that "physics is hard" made some students' initial encounter with physics comprehension challenging.

RELEVANCE IS THE KEY

While there are always some difficulties to be overcome in learning anything new, students are much more willing to expend time and energy when the task at hand can be made relevant to their daily lives. Engaging new experiences that have personal meaning become more attractive and foster persistence. Have you ever tried to crawl on all fours for a few hours at a time? It hurts! Yet babies do it on rugs, hard floors, cement, dirt, and on just about any other surface. Babies are willing to put up with the pain because they have a greater desire to be mobile and explore their world. Mobility is relevant to babies so they deal well with the difficulties of learning to crawl and walk.

PERSONAL MEANING

The same can be said of some of those students who were "failures" in our K–12 schools yet who also were willing to endure the difficulties of re-entering school later in life even when some of them had families and full-time jobs. Why? Because the knowledge or skills they now want have become relevant and very important to their daily lives. Listen to music? Relevancy! Why do so many of our students dislike the classroom situation? It is not relevant to their daily lives. Famed psychologist Carl Rogers similarly reports in *Freedom to Learn*:

> But nearly every student finds that large portions of his curriculum are for him, meaningless. Thus education becomes the futile attempt to learn material, which has no personal meaning.[3]

EXPAND RELEVANCY

Relevance is reinforced when students can see that the topic being discussed also has meaning to their instructor. Students can tell if their physics coach is enthusiastic and involved as well as desiring them to be just as captivated with the subject being taught. Isn't this what we see in good coaches? We observe a kind of single-mindedness that seems to want to draw the athlete into a degree of involvement the same as their coach. A teacher's example is a very powerful testimony as to the value and importance of what they are trying to accomplish.

THE PRESENT

When most of us were students we just did what we were told to do with little sense of purpose except for being constantly reminded that we would need it for our future. When some of us became teachers we realized that planning for the future was important, but neither our students nor we lived there. We lived in the present. Therefore when teaching using this process a key challenge is to make what is being taught relevant to students in their *current everyday lives*. Preparation for the future will naturally occur when the present has meaning. Even if someone teaches a mandatory course, once relevance is established, what is required for the future can soon evolve into what students' desire in the present.

SOME EXAMPLES

Here are a few examples: If you were to teach history, you could start with each student's family tree. You could then go back to the ancestral cultures and show how those effect who each of them has become. If you were to teach English you could begin by teaching your students how to write good notes and e-mails to other students in the class or perhaps text them with proper sentences, spelling, and punctuation. Writing notes and "texting" is what some of them already do, so teach all the rules of good grammar and reading using these relevant vehicles.

DAILY EXPERIENCES

In teaching science using the chemistry of the foods they eat, the physics of the music they listen to, the television they watch, and the computers they use would certainly be appropriate. When students can see the relationships between their time at school and the real things in their daily experiences their learning will stick, not in preparation for testing, but for their personal lives.

FORGIVING LEARNING

I originally experienced this principle from my high school football coach. When I went out for football I wanted to play middle linebacker. To make a long story short, I wasn't very good. But as the season progressed I got better and better. At the end of the season we were going to play our archrival, Antioch. I was put in the starting lineup for the game. My coach played me at first string for the first time that season.

PROGRESS

He *didn't* tell me "You know, Lucido, at the beginning of the season you were lousy but now you're pretty good, so that means you are average and you can't start." No. He looked for progress and where I was at the end of the season in the present moment, not somewhere in the past when the "sins" of my failings were very evident. He forgave my past performances and put them behind us.

HOPE

Surely this story doesn't stand alone in coaching annals, but it brings to light a critically important concept: never take hope away from a learner. None of us wants to be judged by our past failings. Instead we want to be gauged by how those past experiences have given rise to a wiser, healthier, and more competent person in the present. As Thomas L. Good once said,

> As long as students feel there is more risk in making errors than there is payoff in learning, they will remain passive learners.[4]

MIRROR LIFE, NOT THE PAST

During the 2008 Super Bowl the New York Giants played the New England Patriots. The Giants had a 10–6 regular season record and had lost to the Patriots just a few weeks before. The Patriots were 16–0 and a heavy favorite to win. The Giants won the Super Bowl. What was more important is not where either team had been during the season, but where they were at the end of the season entering the Super Bowl. Life is not about the past but about the present moment. Assessments should mirror life. Using Forgiving Learning, no longer is the "test" over and done with and thrown in the garbage can, purged from students' short-term memory. The opportunity to return again and again until comprehension is demonstrated becomes the fertile soil for learning.

FEAR OF GRADES

The last yet most significant anxiety to be addressed was the fear of report card grades. This fear is based on a perceived student lack of control and the possible impact grades could have on their relationship with their parent(s), school activities, insurance/driving licenses, graduation, employment, college acceptance and the like. In the Forgiving Learning process, near the beginning of the year the coach establishes the important classroom atmosphere regarding grades.

REVELATION

Imagine this happening to you: You are awaiting a much-anticipated flight to visit family and friends. You are chatting with others in line about the thrill you get when the plane takes off. Upon being greeted by the flight attendant and having your ticket taken, you randomly glance to your left and a pilot's certificate catches your eye. On a very professional form it says, "This is to certify that Captain John Jones has passed take-offs with a C+, flying with a C, and landings with a D." You stop. A shudder goes through you. The cold hard reality hits home: "This guy hasn't mastered anything about flying this plane. I could die!"

COMPETENCE

How many of us would submit to open heart or brain surgery with a doctor who is average or barely "passed" the class? How many of us would have a home built by a contractor who was "mediocre" in his construction practices? This isn't the way we think. More often than not we assume that, within a range of accomplishment, those we employ to do something for us have achieved a basic mastery and competence in using the necessary skills. This is most often validated by association with one or more master craftsmen/journeymen of that profession as determined by their governing bodies.

MISTAKES

Under the guidance of the master/journeyman, apprentices are given the freedom to make mistakes and then to learn from them so as to enhance their skills and knowledge. Likewise, in order to free students from the fear of grades and scores, the opportunity must be provided for them to repeat assignments and assessments over and over *without penalty* until satisfaction is achieved. During each attempt they should receive directions from the coach as to what they did right, what they did wrong, and how to improve.

FAILURE IS NATURAL

How have human institutions progressed over the millennia? Civilizations, cultures, and individuals have accepted failure as their companion. How frequently does a baby have to fall before it learns to walk? How many failures can it endure? Each iteration brings on a slightly modified new strategy. Is the spirit daunted? Does the baby just give up? Do the parents? On some level both know that success will come eventually and that sufficient failure is needed for walking to take place. The parents know that walking is a natural process. There is no need for punishment to arrive at the desired results. If the baby could talk, all of his/her excuses would be accepted. Persistence would pay off.

RESUBMISSIONS

Consider a structural engineer. When he/she completes a set of drawings and calculations it is submitted to other engineers in the firm for evaluation. It will most often come back "bleeding red" from their comments and critiques. He/she will then rework the plans and resubmit them for scrutiny. This process is repeated many times until the work is approved. The same can be said for newspaper, magazine, and book writing. The editor will ask the author to revise some of the writing many times over before it is acceptable.

FAILURES AND SUCCESS

Over the years we have had many birthday parties with our children. One of the games was to drop the clothes pin into the bottle. Each would take a turn kneeling over the seat of a chair and reaching over the chair's back, aiming and attempting to drop the clothes pin into a wide-mouthed jar. They would shout with glee when they got one in and frown with disappointment when they missed. But shortly after they had completed their turn of clothes pin droppings they would frequently shriek, "Can I do it again?"

ANOTHER TRY

There was no punishment for their failings. They just wanted the opportunity to try again. It was "fun." They had anticipated and accepted that failure could possibly happen and were willing to risk and try again. They were learning something from each miss and wanted to readjust their method and give it another try. Surely their response would have been significantly different if they were punished by having to go to their room after any miss.

ACCEPTING FAILURE

Nearly every night before we go off to bed, a couple of hands of solitaire is played. We have three types that we normally play. It is rare that we win but when we do we slap hands and get a thrill out of it. We accept failure as part of the process. Professional baseball players like to get some kind of a base hit. Even the best of players rarely bats near .400 for a season. That is to say that most of the time a batter makes an out. A good hitter batting .300 makes an out 70 percent of the time and a hit only 30 percent of the time.

EXCUSES

Excuses could abound: "I was fooled," "I swung too soon," "I swung too late." There is a lot of failure in baseball. Why do they still keep coming up to the plate? Each time at bat players have another opportunity to have learned from their mistakes and improve. They have accepted failure as part of the batting process. They transform their reasons for failure, their excuses, into a motivation for progress. It is part of the game:

> I've missed more than 9,000 shots in my career. I've lost more than 300 games, and 26 times I've been trusted to take the game winning shot and missed. Throughout my life and career I've failed and failed and failed again. And, that's why I succeed. —Michael Jordan

USE MISTAKES AND ERRORS

We have not learned this in the game of business or in the game of education. We often see errors and the associated excuses as enemies rather than as friends. Wouldn't it be great to hear a teacher say to a student, "Great mistake! Where did your thinking go wrong? Do you understand your mistake? Do you know what to do if you see this problem again? Okay, now go and give it another try." While this may be the desire on the part of many teachers, their site and district practices and policies may not encourage taking advantage of student mistakes, errors, and excuses as pedagogical tools.

HUMAN CONDITION

Those in education who espouse "No excuses, Just results" do not understand the human condition. Each invention that has advanced civilization has done so on the back of mistakes. Faulty reasoning, design, and construction have plagued human progress since our beginnings. Each error became a stepping stone to the next version of buildings, airplanes, and so many other discoveries. The point is not that we make mistakes, but what we do with them. How do mistakes advance our cause?

> Charles F. Kettering of General Motors once said, "I think it was the Brookings Institution that made a study that said the more educated you were the less likely you were to become an inventor. The reason why is: From the time a kid starts kindergarten to the time he graduates from college he will be examined two or three or four times a year and if he flunks once, he's out. Now an inventor fails 999 times, and if he succeeds once he's in. An inventor treats his failures as practice shots."[5]

DYSON

In 1978, James Dyson noticed how the air filter in the Ball Barrow Spray-Finishing room was constantly clogging with powder particles. So he designed and built an industrial cyclone tower, which removed the powder particles. Could the same principle work in a vacuum cleaner? Five years and 5,127 prototypes later, the world's first bagless vacuum cleaner from Dyson arrived.

RECORDING SUCCESSES AND FAILURES?

Schooling has made it a practice of recording successes and failures. We record those successes and failures as grades and scores. We keep track of them. But it is precisely the reasons behind our successes and failures that take us down the path of growth. Sometimes teachers have had students come to correct conclusions from erroneous thinking. A correct answer seems to be a success. However, when the instructor asks the student for justification, the explanation given may be very inadequate. When we summarize a students' learning with grades and scores, we neglect the most telling part of their story: How did they progress from mistakes and successes to understanding and mastery of the concepts? How they did it is more telling than the end result.

STRENGTHS, WEAKNESSES, AND HOW TO IMPROVE

It does little good for a swimming coach to walk along the edge of the pool and yell "C+ . . . B– . . . C . . . A . . . D" as the swimmer strokes and kicks in her practice laps. To be effective and supportive the coach must talk to her, saying things like, "Dig your hands deeper in the water. Your kick is great. Cup your palms. Okay, now increase your pace." This must be the same protocol used on each academic assignment and assessment tool. If a student can be convinced that errors are to be expected and can be overcome with sufficient practice and without punishment, the resulting effort will prove that their persistence does make a difference.

THE SPOKEN WORD

If you have ever listened to a coach as she speaks to an athlete, you can typically pick up a number of distinct elements: "Adrienne, that was a pretty good dive, but your feet came apart just as you hit the water. Go up and give it another try and this time keep those toes pointed." The first and most obvious observation is that the coach used words, not abstract symbols, to communicate with Adrienne. She gave a personal ("Adrienne") greeting.

QUALITATIVE EVALUATION

She followed with a qualitative evaluation ("That was a pretty good dive, but your feet came apart just as you hit the water.") and concluded with a suggestion for improvement ("Go up and give it another try and this time keep those toes pointed."). The matter was not closed. The evaluation was personal, gave the coach's general response to the dive, and gave directions on how to continue to develop better diving skills.

USE THE WRITTEN WORD

What if you went to your doctor for a physical and at the end of a battery of tests and poking around, she calls you into her office and says, "C+" and walks out. Don't you think you would be pretty upset and probably wouldn't tolerate such a response? Yet many teachers just put a number or letter on an assignment or test and then return it. Fewer write comments throughout the assignment or test. Even a comment like "Well done" is often interpreted by the student as a response to the grade marked rather than the quality of the assignment or assessment.

SEEK IMPROVEMENT

What students, teachers, and parents forget is that the grade, score, or percent written at the top has already terminated the exercise. Even though the assignment is still not completed to the quality required, evaluating it with a number or letter has brought the experience to an end. The student gets the message that this is now done and over, finished. In Forgiving Learning there are no numbers or letters put on any assignment or assessment results. Verbal and written comments affirm what the student has done well, what has been done poorly, and finally what needs to be done to improve the quality to meet the coach's standards.

FROM MEDIOCRITY TO MASTERY

Humans know how to teach humans. What has transpired in the history of education is that teachers continue to accept assignments and assessments from students that are less than what demonstrates satisfactory progress in mastery of the concepts in any course or grade level. We tolerate that which does not convince us that the student really does have a grasp of the tasks at hand. So we satisfy ourselves with less than what is possible and reasonable, just so we can record the assignment with a grade or score and move on to the next topic.

100 PERCENT

This is not the way it is in the real world. Even if you work at McDonald's and are putting together an order for a cheeseburger, fries, and a soda, you cannot ethically demand your salary if you do everything correctly but leave off the cheese. You cannot go to your supervisor and argue that you got 90 percent of the order correct, which is an "A." McDonald's and its customers require 100 percent of the work done as ordered.

RETURNED

This is why in Forgiving Learning when a below par assignment is submitted it is returned to be worked on according to the comments written on the paper. It may have to be done many times over until it is completed to the quality requested. As mentioned earlier, the engineer's designs are often reviewed by other engineers and then reworked over and over until they meet the required specifications. Buildings could fall and people could die if they are just 90 percent correct.

IF YOU DON'T PRACTICE, YOU DON'T PLAY

Most coaches live by this adage. Playing in the game or participating in the match is a privilege and not a right. It is reserved for those who have followed the basic physics' principle: "you can only take energy out of a system if you have first put energy into it." Or in social terms, "you don't get something for nothing." There is merit to the view that being assessed is a privilege reserved for those who have put out the effort and persistence in the learning experience.

REWARDING

It is rewarding for athletes to see how well they can perform in an actual game outside of daily practice sessions. It is rewarding for teenagers to see how well they can drive a car outside of the classroom simulator. It can be very satisfying for students to see how their instructor and/or other evaluators respond to their display of what they have learned. Students will value various types of assessments if they can appreciate that they have worked for the opportunity to demonstrate to themselves and to others how much they have accomplished.

A PRIVILEGE NOT A RIGHT

Following each unit of study there is a student-teacher mastery conference. This is the summative experience in which the student has the opportunity to demonstrate his/her comprehension of the concepts covered. In order to qualify for this conference the students must present a portfolio of all their assignments (all of which will have been completed up to the teacher's standards). In Forgiving Learning the student-teacher mastery conference then becomes the summative assessment medium.

NO PENALTY

But in the Forgiving Learning system, this evaluation is not a "right," it is a privilege for those who have done all the unit assignments to the instructor's standards. If they have not completed their assignments satisfactorily then they can go back and rework them without penalty. If they choose not to take advantage of this option, then they would forfeit the student-teacher conference opportunity and their quarterly or semester evaluation would be diminished for lack of summative information.

STUDENT-TEACHER CONFERENCE

How then does a student come to show mastery of each unit of study? The student must complete each and every assignment to the instructor's satisfaction in order to qualify for the student-teacher conference. Then, in the conference with their teacher, the student proves that he/she has a grasp of the key elements of the unit. The students are expected to demonstrate in some fashion what they know and/or can do.

> "Think of the driving test," said San Luis Obispo High School's English department chair, Ivan Simon. "If you just looked at how well someone answered the written part of the driver's test, then you assume the skill of the driver was represented by only that score. But that person wouldn't necessarily be a good driver."[6]

DEMONSTRATE BY JUSTIFYING ANSWERS

There are no hidden agendas or attempts to use "tricky" questions in the student-teacher mastery conference. A key aspect of each question is the requirement that students justify their answers, that is, explain their thinking or provide some evidence of their understanding. This requires thought and reflective defense of their responses. The conference is held in some isolated part of the room. If students respond to the coach's satisfaction that they have demonstrated mastery of the concept under examination, then the process is repeated for the remaining two or three questions. If they do not master a question they have the opportunity to return at another time to attempt a nuanced form of the same question.

CAN RETURN

They may return as often as they wish at some mutually agreed upon time, with no penalty until they have convinced the coach they understand. Using Forgiving Learning, students' errors are forgiven and they are given other opportunities to demonstrate their understanding. Other options to a student-teacher conference are some type of project or classroom presentation that covers the same concepts. Once again, a weak performance can be repeated at a future time, covering the same learning goals.

QUANTUM LEAP

It is interesting to note that since using this Forgiving Learning process students talk much more about the concepts they have or have not mastered and significantly less about their grades. Students are frequently seen helping each other in talking about these concepts, using everyday examples to illustrate their understanding. Students are seen listening to each other in ways that were extremely rare before.

RESEARCH

Does this kind of Forgiving Learning really produce a quantum leap from "test day learning" to long-term learning? For years a teacher's intuition would say that how a student performed on a test was not nearly as valid as what they had accomplished during the regular part of the course. This sense is supported by the research of Conway, Cohen, and Stanhope in their paper "Why Is It That University Grades Do Not Predict Very-Long-Term Retention?":

> The findings imply that the standard achieved in course work is a more sensitive indicator of knowledge acquisition (and consequent retention) than are examinations. . . . From our studies of cognitive psychology and memory for a work of literature (Conway et al., 1991; Stanhope et al., 1992), it seems clear that examinations are not sensitive to the amount of knowledge acquired. Maybe, as Bahrick (1992) suggested, examination grades are primarily awarded on the basis of knowledge retained in the short term, knowledge that the student rapidly acquired and almost as rapidly lost.[7]

STUDENTS ARE QUERIED

These are physics students' responses to a questionnaire given (after their final grades were recorded) regarding the Forgiving Learning process. It seems to anecdotally corroborate the Conway, Cohen, and Stanhope studies. What follows is a representative sample of what physics students wrote in response to this prompt:

> *Should I use the Forgiving Learning process with student-teacher mastery conferences instead of standard classroom methods using written tests next year? Why or Why not? Do you think you will remember what you've learned more using Forgiving Learning process with student-teacher mastery conferences than tests? Why or why not?*

- "With forgiving learning you retain a lot more because you are talking about what you learn."
- "I think forgiving learning is better because you have to learn it. On tests people cram the night before then forget everything."
- "Definitely!! Do not stop mastery conferences. I have learned so much more this year and I feel like I retain it so much better with masteries. You don't ask us to regurgitate what we've read, but make us apply it to other situations."

- "On a written test we still don't remember everything we did afterwards. Forgiving Learning makes us learn more because we have to know how something works as well as why and be ready for anything."
- "For the written tests I can cram and then forget, but I remember more from forgiving learning conferences."
- "This way you can decide whether we know the concepts and we can't B.S."
- "You get a chance for those who are slow learners to understand the concept."
- "Tests are too impersonal and once we've studied for them and take them we forget them. With forgiving learning on a more personal, one on one basis, allows for better relationship thus allowing, me anyway, to remember the material and I have learned."
- "Forgiving learning conferences are a challenge but you are able to try again which makes it good. I think you will remember more because you are more pressured to learn. If you take a test you could easily copy."
- "When you have forgiving learning there is not a feeling of fear because you can come back. Plus, in a test, if you get it wrong . . . whoopee! You get it wrong and forget about it. In forgiving learning you are forced to learn."
- "I learned more by forgiving learning, it makes me think more and understand better, it's a definite yes. I remember much more with forgiving learning than test. It also improves my ability to speak with others better. It builds my confidence."
- "When you take tests it is just memorizing answers. Forgiving learning is more personal and you have to remember the concepts you have learned, not just memorize them and forget them later."
- "In my particular case, when the word test or quiz or anything of the sort is mentioned something in my brain says, 'forget everything you know!' I tend to worry a lot about my grades and the thought of messing up or in a sense failing scares me a bit. One good thing that I appreciate in Forgiving Learning is the fact that you have the option to come back for as many times as needed and that in a sense I would think it also shows you how dedicated some people are to mastering a unit."
- "Forgiving Learning conferences are an advantage for me because I have time to understand what was taught in that certain unit. It also gives me an idea about how much I really understand. It also helps me with one of my problems; the problem of not being able to explain things to others."
- "Although I am an 'A' student I have grasped all the concepts in physics more so than in any other science class."

- "Simply put, the method that is used to teach this class is, by far, the best that I have encountered in my eleven years of attending school. . . . I honestly believe that the logs have been of utmost importance in increasing the rate of comprehension. . . . I wouldn't revise any part of the system, for I know that I will retain what I have learned longer that anything else I have ever 'mastered.'"
- "The part I like the most about how you teach are the forgiving learning conferences. Because it's not a multiple guess or other written exams where we throw our minds to the paper to pass, it's you who we have to convince we've passed. This makes us study harder and more thoroughly since we don't have an idea of what you are going to ask us. Also, just the thought of an oral exam makes us nervous and so it encourages us to make every effort to answer correctly and support our answers to the best of our ability rather than just remembering the answers and writing them down on a piece of paper. We actually have to think!"
- "Because then you must be prepared for everything."
- "I think you should keep forgiving learning conferences because this way I learn 100%, but in a regular situation I could learn only 90% of the material and still get an 'A.'"

These students were describing what they were experiencing—a kind of learning that would last longer than test-day learning. This was a significant encouragement and validation for the instructional use of Forgiving Learning. This anecdotal qualitative data and the experiences of the previous twenty years of teaching are both convincing and enlightening.

STUDENTS COME FIRST

It showed that learning made more sense to students when teachers stopped marching from topic to topic, chapter-to-chapter quizzing and testing along the way with little regard for the student's true level of comprehension. A coach wouldn't think about introducing an advanced play to the football team unless it could run simpler plays effectively. It made a big difference to stop doggedly following the course outline with more concern for testing than with the healthy progress of students. More important is to focus on teaching students, not a physics course.

ACADEMIC COACHING

Concern for students should come before concern for the topic. Academic coaching meant changing the teaching attitude from classroom manager to professional coach, mentor, and facilitator. It meant using all mustered creativity to teach in a relevant manner. It meant creating a team spirit within the classroom with cooperation winning out over competition.

CHANGE OF ATTITUDE

It involved changing the classroom attitude so that each student could be seen as a person who really wants to know, but who probably has been preconditioned to believe otherwise. The classroom pedagogy should place a higher value on forgiveness and hope than on justice and punishment. If Forgiving Learning was to be effective it must enable students to overcome the fear of their teacher, the fear of the course content, the fear of fellow students, and the fear of their grades. As Carl Rogers said so many years ago:

> Better courses, better curriculum, better coverage, better teaching machines will never resolve our dilemma in a basic way. Only persons acting like persons in their relationships with the students can even begin to make a dent on this most urgent problem of modern education.[8]

ABOLISH HIGH-STAKES TESTS

The greatest walls that confine and limit the true artistic work of teachers are high-stakes tests, grades, and scores. They are the tip of the shark's fin. They are what we see; they are the day-to-day practical extension of the corporate-supported, competitive high-stakes testing system. We have presented rational and effective reasons to support its elimination. As high-stakes tests are abolished, one of the results will be that we will quickly see revealed some of the values that have lain hidden beneath the surface.

> The grading system vitally determines what the teacher will include in his class, what he will omit, and what he will require of students so he can justify the "grade" he must give. The kinds of tests given and how they are graded are often thus determined. Often, the entire system has the effect of so occupying teachers with the necessities of that system, that we often do not permit ourselves to really look at the side effects or consequences of that system.[9]

FORGIVING LEARNING HALLMARKS

The Forgiving Learning process offered here is a brain-compatible solution. Coaches' evaluative interactions with their athletes involve times of encouragement and praise, times of constructive criticism, and times of direction for improvement. This is not accomplished by good wishes, but by intentional classroom design. In summary, the central hallmarks of the Forgiving Learning process include:

- The teacher taking on the mindset of a coach. Enthusiasm for students and topics studied is a key element.
- The learning experience must be designed to maximize student comprehension, not to prepare for external high-stakes testing.
- Content is to be made relevant and meaningful to students.
- Praise, constructive criticism, and suggestions for improvement must constitute the basis for every response to a student's work and assessment.
- Written and/or oral comments must replace scores and grades on all student work.
- Mistakes are a part of the learning process. Accepting errors without punishment must become a common practice in all that students do.
- Requiring that 100 percent of assignments be done with unlimited resubmissions until quality has been achieved is a real life goal.
- Some form of student-teacher mastery conferences, demonstrations, presentations and the like, which provide multiple sources of evidence of what students know and are able to do, is both a valid and a satisfying experience for students and teachers.
- The ability to revisit weaknesses discovered in assignments and during the mastery conferences give the student the sense that forgiveness is real and progress is more important than grades and scores.
- Forgiving Learning must be used as a key component of any grading process, which includes a meeting with students and their self-evaluation.
- Teaming reduces anxiety by changing the relationship with fellow students from that of competitors to a cooperative sense of camaraderie.

NO TO PACING

In today's ordinary classroom a course of study is designed so that it can be completed in a set number of days. With high-stakes testing as the driver, the focus of many classroom activities is "covering" state's academic content standards. Often the lessons are artificially paced so that each is taught in sequence at a specified rate regardless of student comprehension.

NO TO SCRIPTING

In many cases the lessons are scripted for the teachers to follow line by line so that content completion corresponds to district benchmark and/or state testing calendars. The tests become the central concern around which classroom sessions are planned. In this high-stakes testing milieu, many teachers ask the question, "How can I get through the required standards in the allotted number of many so the students will score high on the test(s)?"

HEART OF PLANNING

In Forgiving Learning it is the student, not the testing, that is at the heart of planning each day's activities. The coach (teacher) asks a different question: "How can I organize this experience so that these students will be engaged and masterful learners of the course/grade level standards in classroom time with them?" Topic organization and process is centered on the clientele in the classroom, not testing requirements.

STRENGTHS AND WEAKNESSES

How are these students coming into the classroom? What are their strengths and weaknesses as individuals and as a group? What student differences need to be considered within this context? With this background information the coach begins to address the relational and cognitive needs of each student within the classroom environment. As Albert Einstein said:

> To me the worst thing seems to be for a school principally to work with methods of fear, force, and artificial authority. Such treatment destroys the sound sentiments, the sincerity and the self-confidence of the pupil. It produces the submissive subject. . . . It is comparatively simple to keep the school free from this worst of all evils. Give into the power of the teacher the fewest possible coercive measures, so that the only source of the pupils' respect for the teacher is the human and intellectual qualities of the latter.[10]

NOTES

1. Sidney B. Simon and James A. Bellance, *Degrading the Grading Myths: A Primer of Alternatives to Grades and Marks* (Washington, DC: Association on Supervision and Curricular Development, 1976), 38.
2. American Association for the Advancement of Science. *Project 2061 Science for all Americans* (Washington, D.C.: American Association for the Advancement of Science, 1989).
3. Carl R. Rogers, *Freedom to Learn* (Columbus, OH: Charles Merrill, 1969), 125.

4. Thomas L. Good, "Teacher Expectations and Student Perceptions: A Decade of Research," *Educational Leadership* (February 1981): 415–21.

5. Smithsonian, "Inventors," *Smithsonian*, July 19, 1988.

6. Bryan Dickerson, "This is Only a Test: Are the Stakes Too High for a Flawed System?," *New Times San Luis Obisbo*, August 11, 2005.

7. Martin A. Conway, Gillian Cohen, and Nicola Stanhope, "Why Is It That University Grades Do Not Predict Very-Long-Term Retention?," *Journal of Experimental Psychology* 121, no. 3 (1992): 383–84.

8. Rogers, *Freedom to Learn*, 125.

9. Marshal Fisher, "What's In A Grade," *CSTA Journal* (February 1976): 6.

10. Albert Einstein, *Ideas and Opinions* (New York: Dell, 1981), 69.

TWO

Feelings, Psychological Types, and the Triune Brain

Forgiving Learning continued to be used with much success throughout the 1980s and into the 1990s. This was due in large part to the fact that the process did not stay static. Improvement was sought. In order to move forward there was a need to find out why it worked the way it did. Forgiving Learning originally evolved on gut instincts and past experiences as a student, a teacher, and an athletic coach. But was there something about the makeup of students and teachers that made this process so successful? And if so, could a deeper understanding of why it worked lead to more significant modifications?

USING FEELINGS

Beginning in the 1970s, throughout the 1980s and the 1990s, there were a number of personal experiences that contributed to a clearer understanding of the foundations of Forgiving Learning. It all began with attending a Marriage Encounter weekend in 1973. Its purpose was to deepen and refine couple communication and increased awareness of our values in life. We gained a new insight into the difference between thoughts and feelings and how to use descriptors in explaining them to each other as well as family and friends.

DESCRIBING FEELINGS

We became better able to listen, understand, and experience how each of us felt at various times in our day. The process we learned involved describing our feelings to each other by writing and discussing them. For example, if one of us said, "I *feel* sad," it would be the same as saying "I *am* sad." Saying, "I *think* sad" made no sense. Feelings are intimate and unique to who a person is.

DEEPEN CAMARADERIE

There was a desire to bring this understanding of feelings to the physics students in their classroom teams, which are central in the Forgiving Learning experience. If students could listen and share their emotions with their teammates and their coach, this could deepen the atmosphere of camaraderie and so enhance each student's openness to classroom learning. This insight was to become important as a team classroom culture was being developed. Teaming for students was integral to the classroom learning process and it would later become critical for students with other relational experiences in the worlds of family, friends, school, work, and service.

BRIGGS AND MYERS

While still in the process of understanding and applying each day what had been learned about feelings, in 1975 an introduction came to the psychological typing developed by Carl Jung and employed in the work of Katherine Briggs and her daughter Isabel Myers. Katherine was a pacifist and as WWI came to a close she was trying to develop a psychology that would help bring peace to the world and forestall any future wars.

ENTER CARL JUNG

It was then that she stumbled across the work of Jung who had the answers to her quest. Katherine believed that world peace begins within the family, then moves outward to neighbors, friends, co-workers, local communities, states, regions, and countries. She thought if people really understood how they and others preferred to make decisions, this might encourage a deeper acceptance of self and others.

PSYCHOLOGY AND BRAIN PHYSIOLOGY

Along with feelings, each student's preference in decision making could become a wonderful insight into students' appreciating and cooperating with each other in their classroom teams. Even though they were applying these concepts within the context of the physics classroom, the hope was that it would carry over to their interactions with family, friends, and future co-workers. It was expected that this "soft skill" would become a cornerstone to enhancing student relationships to the benefit of all involved.

> Managers are looking for soft skills over hard skills and social media skills. It's easier for companies to find professionals with the right hard skills, but finding someone who's a good communicator, has emotional intelligence and is able to prioritize work is more challenging. Put yourself into as many social situations as possible; learn to read people, get feedback from your manager and co-workers and work to develop your soft skills. As you move up in an organization, soft skills become more valuable because you'll be managing people and leading them to accomplish goals.[1]

MYERS-BRIGGS SORTER

Over time, Katherine and Isabel collaborated in developing an instrument that would help individuals in understanding their own preferences in decision making. This instrument came to be known as the Myers-Briggs sorter. It was a set of questions that could help students self-identify their "type." Katherine and Isabel first tried the sorter within their family and friends.

WITH CHILDREN

Then in the mid- to late 1950s, needing a larger sample, they sought and received the cooperation of the Philadelphia school district to try the sorter with school children. The results for a student using this sorter was *a beginning* for them to self-determine their preferences and then to use these insights to better understand themselves and others. The central theme here is enhanced communication between each student and others with whom they interact.

STRUCTURE OF TYPES

There are four categories under Myers-Briggs typing. Three of the "preferences" choices (Introversion or Extroversion, Sensing or Intuiting, Thinking or Feeling) came directly from Jung's psychology; the fourth (Judging or Perceiving) was inferred by Isabel and Katherine from Jung's writings. There were no better or worse preferences, just differences from each other. Like feelings, one's preferences have no morality, but what one does with those preferences may.

EITHER/OR

Even though each preference is put in an "either/or" category it does not mean that a student always makes decisions using his/her most inclined preference. It's like left or right handedness. Even though most students are right handed, they may sometimes use their left hands for various activities. A left-handed eater could be a right-handed batter but for most other activities prefer his/her left hand. A preference is just that, that is, the way a student prefers to decide if not coerced otherwise.

FREEDOM

It gives students the freedom to behave contrary to their preference in specific instances, but does not deny their personal proclivities and inclinations. These four preference pairs (I or E), (S or N), (T or F), and functions (P or J) are independent of each other. It works in a manner similar to our bodies. Although we have left or right legs, left or right arms, left or right hands, and left or right feet, each body part can operate independently. But when it is time to run, they coordinate their movements so that sprinting or jogging is possible.

SHORT VERSION

Sometime during the first two weeks of class the students took a short version of this sorter. It was followed up with an explanation of what the sorter results meant and how to use this as a beginning to understand how they choose to make their decisions in life. A presentation was given to the class containing a simple explanation and elaboration on each of the preferences (I, E, S, N, T, F) and overarching functions (J, P) of their best fit type. For the initial step each student ended up with four letters that indicated their preferential tendencies. Further descriptions of the similarities and differences between each of the sixteen combinations of preferences followed.

SELF-SELECT THEIR PREFERENCES

Then after this beginning they were free to select the preference type that they believe best fits them. Clarification was given so that as they began to understand more and more about themselves they may have wanted to reassess their type and select one that is a better fit for them. The emphasis was that it is not outside of their freedom to choose and modify their selection with new insights. The results of the sorter and accompanying specific details gave them a *starting point* and resources to better understand their decision-making process.

NOT A HOROSCOPE

Care was given *not* to make this a "horoscope" type of mentality in which a student's life seems to be determined by the locations of stars and planets. It was further explained that the Myers-Briggs sorter results were a *beginning* for them to understand their own preferences in decision making and how they can still use their free will to go along with their tendencies or behave otherwise. A person can read their horoscope each day in the newspaper and be led to the belief that the outcome of that day will follow a predetermined pattern over which there is no choice. With a horoscope mentality they would see their behavior doomed to their particular preferences without the free exercise of their free will.

SENSING OR INTUITION

In order to make any decision or judgment students must first take in information. Either they prefer to take in information from their five physical senses (sight, hearing, touch, smell, and taste) or through their intuition (inferences that go beyond physical sensations to implications and connections). A student who prefers their senses for input is called a "sensate" (S) and one who prefers their intuition is called an "intuitive" (N). Everyone can utilize either their sensing or intuition when taking in information. But just like right or lefthandedness, they prefer to use one more often than the other.

AN S AND N EXAMPLE

For example, let's say that a couple is at a party. Assume the husband is a sensate (S) and the wife is an intuitive (N). They both spot a couple across the room talking to each other. The husband would just see the facts (S), that is, a man and a woman standing near each other across the room. The wife, while looking at the same couple, might infer (N) either that they are married or perhaps this is their first meeting and they are getting to know each other.

AN APPLE

If someone were to hold up an apple a sensate would say, "Now there is a large bright red apple." An intuitive might say, "Boy . . . that reminds me of my wife's apple pie." A sensate says just what they see with their eyes, whereas an intuitive goes beyond what their eyes see to connections and implications behind the apple. This is one reason that generally intuitive types are better readers. They go beyond the word itself to impressions and extended possible meanings and interpretations.

CLASSROOM APPLICATION

It was obvious to see how important this could be with students' discussions about the process and results of a lab experiment as well as conversations during and after demonstrations and/or content lectures. It is important for students to be able to "see" the world as others do before coming to a team conclusion or resolution. This will help them to recognize that *their* truth is not necessarily *the* truth as they listen to others' opinions and values.

THINKING OR FEELING

After we take in our sensing or intuitive observations (S or N) then a decision can be made by either using the analytical (thinking) logic process (T) or the relational (feeling) logic process (F). One evening a couple was late leaving for a meeting. Their eighteen-year-old daughter, Adri, was seated at the table trying to untangle a necklace. As they were about to leave Adri asked her mother if she could help her with the necklace. The husband said to his wife, "We are late for our meeting. Adri is eighteen. She can handle this. Let's go."

ANALYTICAL/RELATIONAL

The husband's comment was based on *analytical* logic much like Mr. Spock on "Star Trek." His wife, on the other hand, responded to him in a "Mr. Rogers' Neighborhood" manner. She said, "Adri is our daughter. She is asking for help. I will help her." The wife's decision was based on *relational* logic. The wife valued her relationship with Adri in her request for help more than her husband's use of analytical logic to be on time for the meeting. So although they were both faced with the same event (taking in information either through our senses or intuition), each used their preferred type of logic, either analytical (T) or relational (F), to attempt to come to a resolution.

INTROVERSION OR EXTROVERSION

Each student has a preferred comfort zone. For introverts it is in the inner world of reflection and thoughts. For others, like extroverts, it is in the outer world of people and events. So this decision making can take place in either of two places. For the introvert (I) it takes place inside in quiet reflection. For the extrovert (E) it takes place in an outer activity like talking so that the extrovert can process his/her thinking.

AT A RESTAURANT

Let's pretend a wife (an extrovert) and her husband (an introvert) go to a restaurant for dinner. Each is given a menu. The husband quietly reads it over and makes a decision about what he wants. The wife says, "Gee, I don't know what I want. The steak looks good, but perhaps the chicken will be healthier." She might, then, add after looking across to the food on the table next to them comment, "MMMMMMM, that looks wonderful, too." While her husband processes quietly inside (I), she processes outside (E) as she needs to "hear" herself think.

I AND E IN THE CLASSROOM

In the classroom students who most frequently raise their hands to answer a question are usually extroverts. As they talk they are working through the answer and the teacher can hear their thinking process. Introverts tend to not raise their hands. They, too, are thinking of an answer but have little need to say it out loud. The teacher cannot observe their thinking and oftentimes judge that these students do not know the answer because they did not raise their hands.

SUFFICIENCY

While this may be true, it is often a distinct possibility that introverted students do not want to speak out in a large group even if they know the answer. The fact that they have processed their response internally is sufficient. They may also have no need to speak about it for others or for themselves to hear.

UNDERSTANDING AND APPRECIATING

Understanding and appreciating extroverts and introverts is very valuable to student teams. Sometimes students who are introverts are seen by their peers as being "stuck up" or weird because of their preference for silence and lack of expression. They usually have fewer friends, but the relationships are deeper. They prefer to be with one or two others or alone. On the other hand, extroverts are sometimes viewed by their peers as "air heads" who talk a lot, make more commotion, but really say little that is meaningful.

FRIENDSHIPS

Extroverts often have many friends, but the relationships are more superficial. Introverts usually have fewer friends, but their relationships are deeper. Operating within a group of people enhances their style. If students hold onto the derogatory aspects of either of these two preferences (I or E), it can undermine the effectiveness of teamwork and communication.

IT'S PERSONAL

Teachers need to know that when an introvert submits an assignment to the teacher they are submitting a part of themselves; it's personal, it is an extension of who they are. They are saying, "Here I am." Comments or marks on their assignment are experienced as a personal judgment on *them*. But when an extrovert submits a written assignment it is a thing that is outside of them. It is something "other" without personal attachment, that is, "Here is *your* assignment." Comments or marks on their submission are not taken personally but as an evaluation of whatever was submitted.

JUDGING

Finally, there are two overarching functions: Judging (J) or Perceiving (P). Judging student types like to live an orderly, structured life with a focus on bringing decisions to a conclusion as soon as possible either by using their analytical logic (T) or relational logic (F). They seek quick decisions on their activities and exude a confidence in what they arrive at.

PERCEIVING

Perceiving student types like to live by the "seat of their pants" as they put off making a decision while they consider more input and alternatives from either their sensing (S) preference or their intuitive (N) preference. Judging student types have a propensity to make decisions quickly without enough input, while perceiving student types are not quite sure that whatever they decide is correct. They often have lingering doubts.

YES OR NO

When our children were teens they did not like to ask their J type father for permission to go out, fearing their dad would quickly say, "NO." But their mom would usually ask them questions like, "How late are you going to be?" and "Who are you going to be going with?" Then she would often conclude with, "Okay, we'll see." While their father (J) would come to a quick conclusion with little input from them, their mom (P) would be noncommittal in her response as she would ponder options. At least by asking her they had a chance for a positive answer, but with their dad it was quick and dirty—either yes or no.

J/P AND ASSIGNMENTS

J type students have a desire to submit their assignments as quickly as possible with less regard for the quality of their work. P type students often put off completing their assignments on time as they want to do a good job, which takes more time and reflection. It is very important for their coach to consider all types when establishing classroom structure. What must be done to accommodate all preferences? Group work has to be organized so that all students can cooperate effectively in teams. There could be a lot of stress if some members of the team want to hurry up (J) and get a group assignment done, while others want to keep working on it (P).

IN THE OUTER WORLD

In the world outside the classroom, students will be interacting with all types of people and oftentimes may not have a choice with whom they prefer to be involved. But if students know their own personal preferences they will be better able to collaborate with others of similar or differing type. To the extent they can surmise what predilections others may have in decision making they will be better able to communicate effectively with them. It is an invaluable experience to not only value the way fellow students make their decisions, but to respect how others with whom they are in relationship make theirs. This understanding can foster respect and acceptance—two prerequisites of goodwill and harmony in private and public affiliations.

RELATIONAL TONE OF THE CLASSROOM

As we will see later, the learning functions of the human brain are optimized when the "relational tone" of the atmosphere is high: To what degree is there harmony within the classroom teams? The relational tone of the interactions is greatly enhanced when acceptance of all Jungian types is modeled in the structure and operation of daily classroom activities.

TYPE AND LESSON PLANS

Classroom teachers (coaches) will also have their own preferences, but are in a unique position as facilitators of the class. They should not allow personal preferences to dominate their students. They should structure discussions, demonstrations, labs, and other activities to maximize inputs for both sensing (S) and intuitive (N) type students. They should develop explanations that are both very concrete (S), but also contained more subtle elements that resonated with the intuitive (N) types.

FLEXIBILITY WITH J AND P

It is best to establish due dates with flexibility in mind. Perhaps giving a due date for J types to work toward, but also have a window of time (P) where assignments could still be submitted without penalty. Think of saying things like, "This is due on March 3, but you could submit it until March 6 with no consequence." Knowing that they have both introverts and extroverts in their classes should direct coaches to optimize their preferences by having the class divided into small groups (teams) where introverts are more willing to interact and where extroverts are also comfortable.

USING TYPE WITH COACHING

The idea of dividing the class into teams was first created to fit the idea that their physics teacher was going to "coach" the physics class; coaches needed to have a "team." At that time the thinking was not what was best for *them*, but rather what was consistent with the whole coaching idea. But with the understanding of Myers-Briggs student learning styles, it turns out that knowing how to communicate best within a team also satisfies the criteria of enhancing individual student decision-making processes. Wow! What a great two for one.

ACCOMMODATE STYLES

When large group activities are called for the instructor should make sure that introverts could respond to questions either by talking to "their neighbor" (a student next to them) or writing their thoughts. The coach should make it a practice to walk over to a team and ask individuals their thinking about the discussion. Being aware of all the different styles present in the classroom, the coach should be able to accommodate most activities in an attempt to maximize each student's participation.

ENTER LESLIE HART

In 1984 the gift of a book turned out to have a profound effect on what was already in the process of being developed. The name of the book was *Human Brain and Human Learning* by Leslie A. Hart. Resonance was found with much of what had already been done to prepare these physics students to be more responsive to their coach and each other as well as deepening their understanding of physics.

QUESTIONS

Would the ideas of trying to reduce the fears of the teacher, fellow students, the physics content, and grades be supported by this new insight into how a student's brain learns? Would coaching, students working in collaborating teams, learning from mistakes without penalty, sharing and accepting the amorality of feelings, and student learning style preferences find corroboration as being brain "friendly" to students? In summation, would the whole of Forgiving Learning be validated with Leslie Hart's elucidation of brain-compatible learning?

THE BASICS

What was found was that this new brain-friendly model confirmed what this coach's teaching instincts had told him and went beyond that to place these gut feelings on a firm theoretical and practical foundation. We as teachers have as our primary charge the education of our students. What comes immediately to the foreground is that we are primarily involved with each student's brain. For it is in the brain, the integration center for the nervous system, that learning takes place. The brain is the organ for learning just as the heart is the organ to pump blood and the lungs for breathing. So as teachers, if we want to really know how to best teach we need a model that tells us how the brain learns. What follows is a *summary* of this model.

DR. PAUL MACLEAN

Dr. Paul MacLean, the former director of the Laboratory of the Brain and Behavior at the United States National Institute of Mental Health, developed this model of the brain based on its evolutionary development. It is referred to as the "triune brain theory" because MacLean suggests that each student brain is actually three brains in one. Each of the layers or "brains" was established successively in response to evolutionary needs. The three layers are the *reptilian brain,* (reptilian *complex*), the *limbic system* (old mammalian brain), and the *neocortex*. Each layer is geared toward separate functions of the brain, but all three layers interact substantially. [1]

THE REPTILIAN COMPLEX

The student's reptilian complex consists of the brain stem and the cerebellum (see the *Primitive Brain* in figure 2.1). Its purpose is closely related to actual physical survival and maintenance of the body. The cerebellum orchestrates student movement. Digestion, reproduction, circulation, breathing, and the execution of the "fight or flight" response during stress are all housed in the student's reptilian complex.

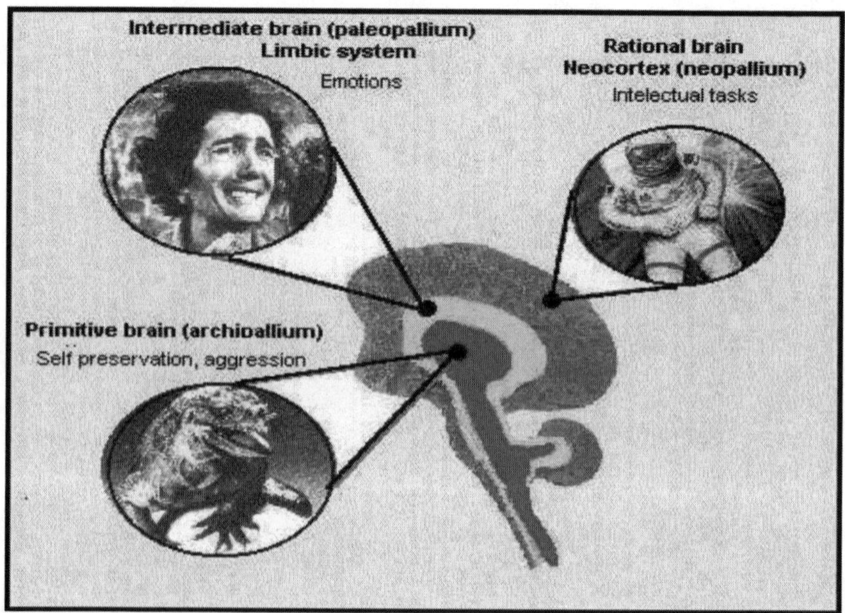

Figure 2.1. Illustration from Júlio Rocha do Amaral and Jorge Martins de Oliveira, *The Three Units of the Human Brain*, http://www.cerebromente.org.br/n05/mente/limbic_i.htm

SURVIVAL

Because the reptilian brain is primarily concerned with physical survival, the student behaviors it governs have much in common with the survival behaviors of animals. It plays a crucial role in establishing home territory, reproduction, and social dominance. The overriding characteristics of student reptilian complex behaviors are that they are automatic, have a ritualistic quality, and are highly resistant to change.

THE LIMBIC SYSTEM

The student's limbic system or old mammalian brain, the second portion of the brain to evolve, houses the primary centers of emotion. It includes the amygdala, which is important in the association of events with emotion, and the hippocampus, which is active in converting information into student long-term memory and in memory recall. Repeated use of specialized nerve networks in the hippocampus enhances memory storage, so this structure is involved in student learning from both commonplace experiences and deliberate study. However, it is not necessary for a student to retain every bit of information learned.

RELATIONAL NEEDS

The amygdala comes into play in situations that arouse student feelings such as fear, pity, anger, or outrage. Because the student's limbic system links emotions with behavior, it serves to inhibit the reptilian complex and its preference for ritualistic, habitual, or impulsive ways of responding. The student's limbic system is also involved in activities related to bonding and relational needs, as well as behavior related to expression and mediation of emotions and feelings, including emotions linked to attachment. These protective, loving feelings become increasingly complex as the limbic system and the neocortex link up.

THE NEOCORTEX

The student's neocortex, also called the cerebral cortex, comprises five-sixths of the human brain. It is the outer portion of the brain and is approximately the size of a newspaper page crumpled together. The neocortex makes language, including speech and writing, possible. It allows logical and formal operational thinking and lets students look ahead and plan for the future. The neocortex also contains two specialized regions, one dedicated to voluntary movement and one to processing sensory information.

INTERCONNECTEDNESS

All three layers of the student's brain interact. They are connected by an extensive two-way network of nerves. On-going communication between the neocortex and the limbic system links thinking and emotions; each influences the other and both direct all voluntary action. This interplay of memory and emotion, thought and action is the foundation of a student's individuality. The full extent of this interconnectedness is unclear. However, it is entirely incorrect to assume that in any situation one of our three "brains" is working and the others are not. What we can do, tentatively, is assume that at times one particular focus may be dominant while the rest of the brain acts in support and that education can influence which focus dominates.[2]

JUNG MEETS MACLEAN

The Jungian *psy*chology, as refined by Myers and Briggs, fits perfectly into Dr. Paul MacLean's *phys*iology of how the human brain learns best. It is within the old mammalian portion of the brain (or limbic system) that a student assesses the relational tone of the classroom environment. If the situation is positive, it permits the neocortex to operate at a higher level and if not, it *downshifts* to the reptilian portion of the brain that engages a fight or flight response.

THREATENED

Students learn best when the neocortex is engaged at a high efficiency in thinking and doing. When students feel threatened their neocortex downshifts to the reptilian brain's fight or flight instincts. It does this in order to minimize anticipated harm by mentally *escaping* the classroom to be "safe." This "escape" is the reduced functionality of thinking and processing in the neocortex. Students cannot learn well with a low-functioning neocortex.

AMORALITY

So in order to engage the neocortex, students do have to experience a sense of peace and good relationships with those with whom they are interacting. This begins with the satisfaction of understanding their own preferences and proclivities in decision making. This will help them to appreciate others with whom they are relating. Simplified: an "I'm okay, you're okay" attitude is a healthy thing to develop among students and teachers alike. This includes the amorality of both their Jungian decision-making process and their feelings as well.

FROM PROTECTION TO RISK

Although the student brain is the organ for learning, it does so with some caution as with the signal of a flashing yellow light rather than an immediate green one. Student brains are preset from birth to prevent them from learning something new without some reflection. All of the input senses enter the reptilian complex first before going to the neocortex where students think. It asks these questions: Will learning this harm me? Should I run? Should I fight? Is it worth the chance to step out and give it a chance or just stay where I am and be comfortable and free from possible harm? Teachers and students should sometimes risk doing innovative and creative things, not rehash what was already done.

FEAR REVISITED

Earlier in this work students' fears of their teacher, fellow students, the physics content, and grades were described. Fear can be described as the anticipation of future pain. A student's reptilian brain wants to avoid feelings of fear in anticipation of bad things happening. Following its natural tendencies students' brains downshift to "reactive survival mode." As teachers and learners we should not be reluctant to try something we have not done before. Being creative and innovative sometimes involves risk taking. So how can students circumvent the brain's natural tendency to be fearful of new experiences?

MINIMIZING THE DOWNSHIFT: CAMARADERIE

Students need to know that there are some things that they can do to minimize the impulse to flee learning situations that they may judge as threatening, which will trigger the brain to downshift from the neocortex (where learning takes place) to the reptilian complex's protect and escape. First is to overwhelm the anticipation of future fear with the anticipation of future pleasure. There is pleasure in healthy camaraderie—especially if there is a history of positive supportive interactions with teammates. The classroom pedagogy must reinforce collaboration with other students. Doing this will enhance the relational tone so individual students will not feel alone in the new learning endeavor.

MINIMIZING THE DOWNSHIFT: NOT ALONE

When students believe that they are in an academically fearful situation alone, their anxieties increase. It's just like walking down a dark street at night all by oneself. It can be scary. If a person had a cadre of friends as well as a police officer alongside their concerns would be diminished. With Forgiving Learning students have cultivated a team of classroom friends who can help clarify and explain the area(s) of confusion to their satisfaction. While there is no police officer in the classroom, there is a coach who is on their side and will do whatever is necessary to bring light to areas of darkness in comprehension. Students should be able to reflect on the pleasure of such a positive support system when fear creeps in.

MINIMIZING THE DOWNSHIFT: REDEEMABILITY

Secondly the ordinary classroom situation is predicated on assignments and assessments being submitted, graded, or scored and then recorded. But with Forgiving Learning, assignments and assessments can be done over and over until completed satisfactorily. Students do not have to fret that all submissions are of a one-and-done variety, but rather all their classroom shortcomings are redeemable. This knowledge has the potential of bringing peace and satisfaction, thus reducing associated worries and fears.

CORNERSTONE

When students realize that this Forgiving Learning is not some arbitrary accommodation but the cornerstone of how the classroom operates, it brings confidence and hope. This can again minimize anticipated fears and permit student learning in a positive and supportive atmosphere. So as not to overwhelm both coach and student with redone assignments and assessments their number should be kept to the minimum required to effectively address the classroom goals. It takes practice to determine what both students and instructor can reasonably handle. Coaches need to return evaluated assignments and assessments in a timely manner so that students get feedback as soon after completion as possible.

MINIMIZING THE DOWNSHIFT: SMALL BITES

Third there is the memory of watching a mother feed her very young children. If she put the food in their mouths too quickly after the initial bite they would spit it out. But a little food at a time and at the pace that each child wanted worked the best. So it is with a student's brain. Give it *a little at a time* so as not to overwhelm it, thus preventing it from downshifting into reactive survival mode.

COMFORT ZONE

Students live in a space some call the comfort zone. If they want to learn something new beyond this comfort zone they have to step out of this space to try something new. This can be called the learning zone. Students should not step out too far. If they take too big a leap they will enter a confusion zone. When overwhelmed the neocortex will downshift to the survival mode of the reptilian brain and learning will be reduced. So when coaches are designing a new experience for their students it must be enough to encourage student engagement while monitored for its appropriateness for their success.

MINIMIZING THE DOWNSHIFT: SUCCESSFUL PROGRAMS

The brain works by using programs it stores for future use in similar situations (biases). When a program works properly and success is achieved, natural pleasure is the result. Think of a basketball player whose brain has a program to shoot the basketball into the hoop. When the program works (the ball goes through the hoop), the neocortex is flooded with hormones (called endorphins) that give the person a pleasurable feeling.

FEEDBACK

In a similar fashion the coach can ask simple questions that allow each student to respond orally or perhaps on a handheld white board or electronic device. In this way the coach and fellow teammates can give immediate responses to each other. The sooner students' brains get feedback the quicker their successful programs can be affirmed, modified, or retried for confirmation. This will build confidence and persistence in learning something new. Experiencing successful programs prevents downshifting into the reptilian brain's reactive survival mode, which minimizes the learning that takes place in the neocortex.

MINIMIZING THE DOWNSHIFT: STUDENTS HAVE A SAY

In the classroom setting, students' anticipation of future failure can also be a source of significant anxiety. When students believe that the evaluation of their success is outside of their influence, it raises this anxiety, which is a gateway to uncertainty and downshifting. In Forgiving Learning students are provided the opportunity to rework assignments and assessments until completed to their instructor's satisfaction. This encourages persistence in learning and gives them some measure of control.

OVERCOME FEAR

Students know that they are responsible for their success as they continue to have the opportunity to again and again address their shortcomings. If we add to this the opportunity to contribute to their summative evaluations (in most cases, their report card grades), the anticipation of future failure can be further diminished. Thus hope can overcome fear and keep the neocortex engaged in learning.

REFLECT AND EVALUATE

Academic coaching, like athletic coaching, provides the opportunity to assess and communicate to students their strengths, weaknesses, and suggested paths to improvement. Students are not inanimate objects but human beings who can reflect and evaluate their own perception of learning or lack thereof. After all, their brains' programs, which are the result of their learning, do reside within them. This means that students can contribute to their evaluation by articulating their own understanding.

EVALUATION CONFERENCES

For this they need a forum. What coaching in the Forgiving Learning classroom does is establish regular meetings with individual students during which they have the opportunity to describe how they have engaged in activities such as planning how to approach a given learning goal, monitoring comprehension, and evaluating progress toward the completion of a task. These conferences should be planned once or twice a quarter.

STUDENTS' SELF-EVALUATION

How each teacher takes this into consideration is left up to individual instructors with the caveat that students need to know how their self-evaluation contributes to the final mark. As the instructor of record the instructor is responsible for arriving at and recording their official report card grade. How those grades are "produced" should include telling students what has been seen as their strengths, weaknesses, and paths to improvement.

SOLID FOUNDATION

There was more to the idea of Forgiving Learning than had originally met the eye. It worked because there were some psychological and physiological principles that were at the heart of its operation. It was only after some personal experiences that this came to light. The nature and value of students sharing feelings as well as the importance of understanding and appreciating Jungian types shed light on enhancing student relationships and the efficacy of teams. When this is combined with brain-compatible classroom pedagogy Forgiving Learning is set on a solid foundation. The human brain is the organ for student learning. The critical function of the student's neocortex is the acquisition of useful programs. This acquisition is called learning.[3]

CLASSROOM BIAS

The ordinary bias (atmosphere or location) for this learning is within the context of the classroom. The more learning can take place outside of the classroom bias the more these programs will be usable in each student's life in the world beyond the school setting. School is an artificial environment that hopes to prepare students for engagement in life outside of its purview. While within the context of the classroom the student is not alone. The facilitator of this learning is the student's academic "coach" (teacher or instructor). Alongside of each student are others on a like mission: to learn. While provided with adequate materials and supplies within a safe and healthy environment, the student's coach has the mission of providing those experiences that will facilitate this learning.

LIMBIC SYSTEM

The coach must know how students learn best. Essential to this is the physiology and psychology of the student's brain. Access to the neocortex is through the limbic system (the old mammalian brain). When students feel safe and are in a relationally positive environment (cooperative teammates and instructor), conditions are prime for learning. When students are fearful or anxious the brain downshifts to the old reptilian brain, which focuses on protection and escape. Avoiding this downshift is a prime directive for classroom structure and operation.

FURTHER VALIDATION: MASLOW

As if this is not enough theory and practice to have confidence in the efficacy of Forgiving Learning, we can consider the contributions of

Abraham Maslow's hierarchy of needs. Surprisingly and perhaps embarrassingly, the work of Maslow was not employed during the inception and development of Forgiving Learning. It was only afterward in reflection that there was an "aha" experience of a memory of being introduced to Maslow in an undergraduate course in educational psychology. His model of a human's hierarchy of needs (depicted in figure 2.2) is especially relevant in education as it is students who are the focus of our attention.

PSYCHOLOGY MEETS PHYSIOLOGY

The first and most primal of psychologist Maslow's hierarchy of needs are physiological. As applied to students, they have a physical need for oxygen and food as well as management of bodily functions such as heart rate, blood circulation, breathing, digestion, and other related basic life maintenance requirements. These are all managed by the reptilian brain of Dr. MacLean's triune brain model.

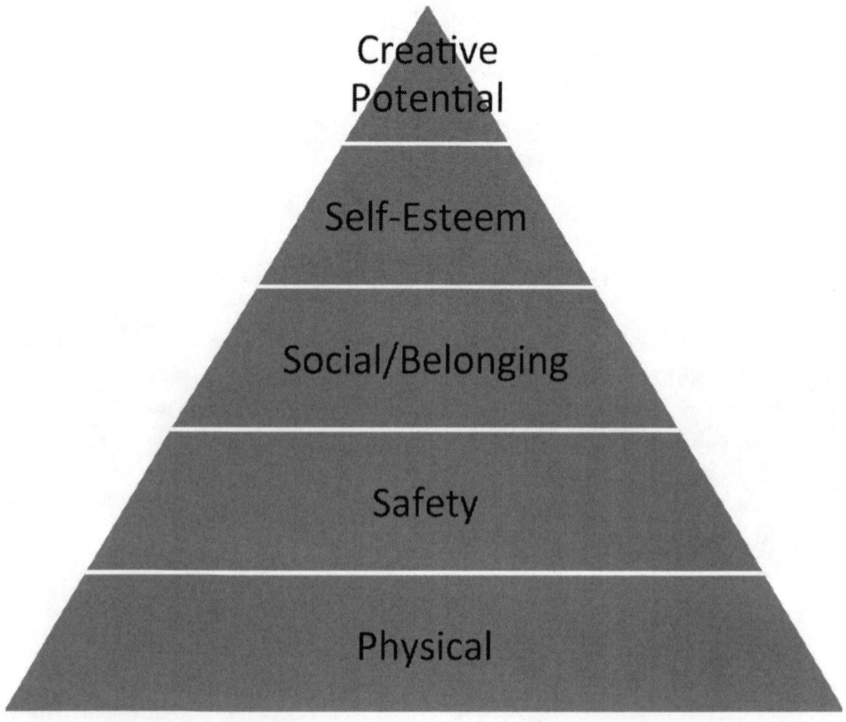

Figure 2.2.

VALIDATION

Not only that, but the second of Maslow's needs related to the first is for safety and security sometimes called instincts. This, too, is a prime directive of the reptilian brain, which also is responsible for fight or flight actions when threat is present. So what we have here is a validation that Maslow's first two human needs are really the responsibility of the reptilian complex of Dr. MacLean's triune brain model.

LIMBIC SYSTEM AND BELONGING

To go further, Maslow's third set of needs is for love and belonging. It reveals our students' need for an atmosphere of care and affection. We have described earlier that in order for the neocortex to operate well the student's old mammalian brain (limbic system) must be able to first survey the environment and deduce that it is conducive to peace and harmony. When there are positive, supportive relationships between students (including the instructor), the limbic system provides the stimulus for the neocortex to function well. This is why working as teammates is so valuable to the learning environment.

SEEKING ESTEEM

It is within the context of classroom interrelationships that the student can experience the last pair of Maslow's needs: self-esteem and receiving the esteem of others. Both of these can be found in appropriate team activities where individuals are given the opportunity to affirm their own and each other's qualities by offering honest praise, admiration, and respect. While these should be a frequent part of each student's home family system, it is a regular part of Forgiving Learning's classroom pedagogy.

REGRESSION

Just as a student's brain downshifts when frightened from the neocortex to the reptilian brain and its "survival reactive mode," Maslow held that when under stressful conditions students can regress to a lower "need" level. So if a student's esteem is damaged by a poor initial performance on an assignment or assessment he/she will regress to the lower level need for the comfort of love and belonging of friends and/or family. Thus "regression" to a lower need level for Maslow is akin to the brain "downshifting" when under threat to fight or flight for protection. In both cases students seek escape to "lick their wounds."

CREATIVE POTENTIAL/SELF-ACTUALIZATION

Once the four basic survival/health needs (physiological, safety, love, and esteem) are in various stages of being addressed, there arises within students a greater and greater desire for intellectual, emotional, psychological, and spiritual growth. This final step in the hierarchy of needs Maslow calls self-actualization. Here students experience confidence and competence in who they are and what they are about. Students move through these five levels in stages. Like newborns, their needs are primarily physiological.

NURTURING FOR GROWTH

Then as they begin to interact with their environment they recognize that they need to be safe. Soon students seek out attention and affection from those around them. As growth and development continue students desire esteem from themselves as well as others. While all these four essential needs are present from birth, there is an ebb and flow between them even on a daily basis. While interacting with other students and their coach in the classroom can begin to satisfy some aspects of these needs, it is the whole circle of family, friends, and extended community that becomes the fundamental nurturing environment for growth.

NOW WHAT?

Resting on the shoulders of these personal experiences with feelings, psychological preferences, and brain-compatible learning, the Forgiving Learning pedagogy is clearly supported by the educational applications of Jung, Myers and Briggs, MacLean, Hart, and now Maslow. With this solid foundation we will now turn to the practical aspects of how to initiate, nurture, and personalize Forgiving Learning in the K–12 classroom.

NOTES

1. Brazen Careerist, "Central Valley Marketplace," *Fresno Bee*, May 11, 2014.
2. Brazen Careerist, "Central Valley Marketplace," *Fresno Bee*, May 11, 2014.
3. Renate Nummela Caine and Geoffrey Caine, *Making Connections: Teaching and the Human Brain* (Nashville, TN: Incentive Publications, 1990).

THREE

Setting the Stage for a Relational Classroom

The Forgiving Learning pedagogy does not just mysteriously "happen" because it is intellectually understood by the classroom instructor. Concrete practices and policies must be established to create a new classroom culture. Its operation is not accidental but a deliberate and planned process. Students must be made ready to participate in this new structure. The application of Forgiving Learning strategies discussed in the ensuing chapters must be adjusted and modified for each grade level/age group to be developmentally and culturally appropriate.

GENERIC

It is under the professional expertise of each teacher that these alterations are to be made. Differences in prevailing classroom ethnic cultures may play a part in any reconstitution of the suggestions presented in this work. Forgiving Learning may look quite different in predominately Native American classrooms as it would with a significant Hispanic or Asian influence. What is presented here is what can be considered a "generic" brand, although surely impacted by this coach's personal history.

MODIFICATIONS

It is also true that each instructor is given a measure of academic freedom depending on the educational philosophy of his/her state, district, school site, and associated administrators, laws, and regulations. It is important that once the Forgiving Learning paradigms are accepted by the classroom professional that each teacher finds the space within their employment limitations to include those lesson portions that they believe are most meaningful to their students' classroom experience. It is not wise for teachers to jeopardize their teaching vocations using an all or nothing mentality. Instead, they should determine what is doable in their circumstances and do it well.

SETTING UP THE NEOCORTEX

When students enter the classroom the teacher assumes that their needs for food, shelter, health, and safety are being met both at home and by school site programs. Remember that the reptilian portion of each student brain will stimulate the student to satisfy these needs before they will be open to learning. Students will not effectively be able to engage their neocortexes to "think" (develop successful programs that we call learning) without these necessities.

RELATIONAL TONE

Next in line to survey the environment is the old mammalian portion of the brain or the limbic system. It is here where the relational tone of the environment is assessed for harmony and a positive experience with others with whom the students are relating. This old mammalian brain is the final doorway to the neocortex. This chapter presents a set of experiences that are directed to satisfy the needs of the old mammalian brain or limbic system. The stage will then be set for learning.

RATIONALE

Often students do not see the rationale for peculiar activities that instructors have planned for them. This is more evident as students proceed from elementary school on to middle and even more so in high school. In an attempt to minimize resistance to cooperating with the suggested activities the teacher can tell them the story of the 1984 movie *The Karate Kid.* Some may have seen the original and can help the coach along in the story telling. One teenager Daniel La Russo has recently moved to Los Angeles from New Jersey with his mother.

A NEW STUDENT

While in New Jersey he had picked up a book on karate and had begun to teach himself some of the techniques. While resistant to leave New Jersey he cooperates with his mom and their new life. As a new student at the local high school, he meets an attractive girl in his class but is unaware that she is spoken for by the leader of a blond surfer group. Even with some regular taunts by members of this group (who also belong to a local karate school or dojo) he is able to avoid fighting by not provoking them.

HALLOWEEN DANCE

But at the school's Halloween dance he encounters a few of the surfers in the bathroom who are smoking in one of the stalls. As a payback for their harassment of him he uses a nearby janitorial hose to soak the stall and then jumps on his bike to escape home. As he approaches his apartment complex with the other teens in hot pursuit on their motorcycles he rides up to the cyclone fence with the intent of climbing over it. No sooner than reaching the fence Daniel is caught by the group. Then, in quick succession, one after the other of the six dojo members pummel him with karate blows that bring him to his knees.

MR. MIYAGI

Then as the leader is about to hit him with one final and potentially lethal coup de grace the scene shows a small man climbing over the fence from the apartment side. Within a few minutes he quickly outfights and dispatches all six of them, puts Daniel over his shoulder, and climbs back into the apartment complex. The man who came to Daniel's rescue turns out to be the apartment gardener and repairman, Mr. Miyagi. Once Daniel realizes what had happened he implores Miyagi to help him learn karate so that he can protect himself. Although at first reluctant, he relents and tells Daniel to come to his home the next day to begin his training.

WAX ON/WAX OFF

When he first comes to Mr. Miyagi's home he is met with a small fleet of vintage cars. He is told to begin by washing the cars. After he is done he is directed to wax each one. When he begins to apply the wax, Mr. Miyagi stops him and directs him to move the cloth in his hands in circular motion to apply and then remove and polish with the cloth using the phrase, "Wax on, wax off." Although appearing a bit confused Daniel follows directions and then is told by Miyagi to return the next day. When Daniel arrives the next day Mr. Miyagi brings him into his backyard, which is covered with myriad wooden walk ways and demonstrates to him how to "sanda floor" by repeated horizontal strokes while on his knees. Daniel is exhausted at the end of the sanding experience and Miyagi tells him to return the next day.

PAINTING

Arriving early he is met with a large can of paint and two paint brushes, one for each hand. He is shown all the extensive fencing surrounding the yard and told to paint successive boards painting downward with one brush and upward with the other. After some coordination flubs he begins the task. When complete he leaves for home without any discussion with Miyagi. The next morning he is met with more cans of paint and brushes and a note to him. Mr. Miyagi declares that he has "gone fishing" and told Daniel to paint the horizontal slats covering the house using horizontal strokes like the vertical ones of the fence.

"SANDA" FLOOR

When Miyagi returns from his fishing trip, Daniel is not only exhausted but fed up too. He confronts Miyagi and yells at him, "Look! I came here to be trained for karate and all you have had me do is to wash and wax your cars, sand the floors, paint the fence and now the house, I have had it . . . I quit." In a very powerful moment, Miyagi, standing right in front of Daniel, shouts back at him, "Daniel-son, sanda floor." Confused and caught off guard he begins to bend down and kneel on the deck. Miyagi stands him up and begins to throw karate blows at him as Daniel now uses his sanding strokes to block each punch. Then Miyagi continues with other karate strokes, which Daniel is able to successfully counter with all the movements he used to sand, paint, and wax.

MASTER

Daniel finally gets it. Although he did not know that he was actually in training with all the waxing, sanding, and painting he now could see the reasoning the karate master, Mr. Miyagi, was using. The first was to be disciplined and obedient to his master teacher in his training as he does not yet understand all there is to becoming well schooled in karate. The second is that all that may be asked for may not be as it appears. Miyagi is asking Daniel to trust him that whatever he directs him to do is for his own good in becoming a karate expert. After telling this story and its meaning the classroom "coach" now asks the students to trust that all the different things that will be asked of them has purpose to their learning. The value of each will be revealed in time when appropriate.

PURPOSEFUL ACTIVITIES

Students who care for and respect themselves become less defensive and thus more open to appreciate other students and more willing to learn. The more threatened students are the more they will focus on survival and less on relating positively to their immediate environment. What follows is a set of purposeful activities that address student-student and instructor-student interactions. It is strongly suggested that you initiate the school year with a series of experiences to begin to develop bonding and networking among the students and yourself.

ALLOW TIME

Allow the class two to three weeks for students to assimilate this introductory "Forgiving Learning" mindset into their school experience. You may have other like activities or modifications that better fit your classroom situation. Some elements of these activities should be continued on a regular basis throughout the year. For example, the first five minutes of each day, every Wednesday for ten minutes, etc. Spontaneous inclusion should not be so far separated during the course/grade level as to prevent a sense of continuity. Putting aside time for these experiences tells the students that you value them and these aspects of their education.

a. Stereotypes
b. Negative criticism
c. Thoughts vs. feelings
d. Opinions vs. values
e. Dealing with mistakes
f. Affirming self and others
g. Hearing vs. listening
h. Body language
i. Checking for understanding

STEREOTYPES

Okay, let's begin by looking at how students deal with others when they pigeon hole them because of specific characteristics. This will reveal how stereotypes affect a student's self-perception and behavior with others. It is also a good opening exercise because it is fun and opens the kids to you and to each other. Be careful not to choose students who appear to already be living out a stereotype that matches the part they will enact in the exercise.

RANDOM LABELS

Let them know that these labels are being assigned randomly and have nothing to do with students' actual attributes. In this role play each student in the group is to try to figure out what stereotype they represent by how others in the group are treating them. Each student's stereotype and how others in the group would commonly treat them will be on a folder label stuck to their foreheads (it sticks easily and is easily removed). Ask for six volunteers to be in the role play. Beforehand the teacher is to prepare these six stickers:

Brain—respect me
Nerd—mock me
Cheerleader—sweetly tolerate me
Jock—fearfully include me
Bully—disregard me
Learning disabled—help me

THE COMMITTEE

Once the six are assembled tell them that they represent a committee of students who are to plan an end-of-the-year party for the class. They are to sit in a circle of chairs/desks with the rest of the class surrounding them. Next go to each of the six students and apply the stickers to their foreheads. The class is to be instructed to just listen, make no comments or try to give clues as to what any forehead sticker says.

ORGANIZE

The committee can organize themselves however they want but their goal is to come up with a workable plan, all the while each individual will be internally trying to figure out what the stereotype sticker on their forehead says. Once the committee's plan is completed the teacher is to give each student in turn the opportunity to guess what their sticker says and how they came to that conclusion and what it felt like to be treated like that. Ask the others how they felt about treating others according to the labels on their foreheads.

NEGATIVE CRITICISM

In this classroom experience we want our students to internalize what happens when students make comments or gestures that are intended to reject another student's ideas, opinions, values, feelings, or dreams. For this exercise the teacher will break the class up into groups of three to five each. It works best if each group can sit around a common table or desk. Each group will need one piece of 8 1/2" x 11" paper, some coloring pens and/or pencils, one pair of scissors, and transparent scotch tape.

GROUP DIRECTIONS

The directions for each group are to create and name a "doll" of their own choosing, color it, and then cut it out. The doll should be about the size of the paper. Each person must have some input into the shape, size, coloring, etc. of the doll. Each should say in turn what they are doing and why, for example, "I am drawing the hair black because . . ."and so forth for each person. After each group is finished and had named their doll they are to pass it from person to person in their group so that each in turn could cut out some part of the doll.

NAMED, CUT, AND TORN

Once the doll is finished being named and cut out, each person in turn is to hold the doll in his/her hands and verbally criticize some aspect of the doll by first calling the doll by name followed by a negative comment, for example, "Sara Lou, your hands are lumpy!" Following this they are to tear off that portion of the doll that best represents their criticism. They must then keep that torn off portion of the doll in front of them as they pass the remaining part of the doll to the next student. After each person in turn has critiqued and torn off a piece of the doll and placed it in front of them, the remaining portion of the doll is to be placed in the center of the table/desk.

APOLOGIZING

The students then go back around the group, this time each in turn apologizing for their comment and their tearing off of the offending part, for example, "Sara Lou, I'm sorry. You really do have nice hands." They follow up their apology by taping the very piece they had torn off back on the doll on the back side so the tape cannot be seen from the front. They are then to discuss how the doll looks now as compared to how it looked when they began and what message they got out of this experience.

SUMMARIZE AND DISCUSS

Summarize comments from each group for the whole class and discuss the deleterious effects this kind of talk can have on group interactions.

Even though the doll may look pretty much the same after the taping back of the torn portions, there are still scars that may not be able to be seen from the front. After all the students in the circle have apologized and "repaired" the doll, the students are then to discuss how the doll looks now as compared to how it looked when it was first drawn, and what message they learned out of this experience. The only way to be sure not to emotionally injure someone is not to do it in the first place. Students are reminded to be conscious of all they say and do to their fellow students.

THOUGHTS VS. FEELINGS

In this experience students will learn how to distinguish feelings from thoughts and how to effectively describe them and respond to others' expressions of emotions. When students come into our classrooms they, like us, are filled with feelings. If we can open the door to us and our students accepting each other's emotions this can foster a much healthier classroom atmosphere. The more relationally comfortable students feel, the more able the old mammalian brain is to then support the neocortex as it engages in the learning endeavor. Before beginning the actual exercise, the instructor should read and formulate a way of having students understand the following feeling and thinking concepts.

I AM, I FEEL

Feelings describe the most intimate and deepest part of us and our students. When a student says, "I feel sad," they could have easily said, "I am sad." This is who I am right now . . . sad. A feeling is not a glib literal expression, but rather reveals something much more personal than our thoughts. It makes no sense to say, "I think sad." There is much confusion in our everyday lives about the difference between thoughts and feelings.

SOFT SKILL

While we may not bring it to our consciousness, our capacity to really listen to another person's feelings can hold the key to a deeper and more wholesome relationship. As we try to develop a Forgiving Learning culture in our classrooms, the description and acceptance of feelings among students and between ourselves and our students will go a long way in fostering a positive relational tone. This ability or "soft" skill is not just of benefit to school-age children. As they mature and grow it will be of great advantage in their interactions with family, friends, and co-workers.

NO MORALITY TO FEELINGS

To begin with, feelings are neither right nor wrong—they are amoral. There is *no morality* to feelings, they just are. Feeling happy or sad, joyful or depressed are all amoral equivalents. It is our *behavior* that can be considered good or bad. If a student says "I feel jealous," there is nothing wrong with that. But if a student rejects another person or decides to do them some verbal or physical harm they then enter into the realm of morality.

JEALOUSY

The feeling of jealousy resides within and is just that, a feeling. We don't know where it comes from nor is it necessary or possible to "figure out" its history or origins. The same set of circumstances can stimulate different feelings in different people. Saying something in class that some in the class consider funny and have laughed at may also have elicited sneers from others.

I THINK VS. I FEEL

What is important is that we need to listen to others' feelings differently than their thoughts. If someone were to say "I *feel that* it is cold in here," they have expressed a *thought,* not a feeling. They could just as easily said "I *think* that it is cold in here" and the sentence would have made sense. *Feel that* means *think that*. Because they expressed a thought you could easily take issue with them and say, "I think that the temperature is just fine." Now if instead they said "I *feel* cold," who can take issue with how you are feeling? Whether anyone else likes it or not, this is how you are feeling. The response that is rarely heard is, "Tell me what it is like to feel your kind of coldness."

DESCRIBING FEELINGS

In other words, when fellow students express their feelings the most we can do for them is to tell them we are open for them to tell us more about their feelings—to *describe* it for us so that we can better empathize with them. How often will a parent, teacher, or other student ask you how you are feeling today? How quickly some respond by saying "Fine, just fine," when in reality they could be sad, depressed, or elated.

REJECTION

Most of us don't really believe that someone cares about our feelings, nor are we prepared to describe to another person how we are really feeling. This is because we don't know what they will do with our feelings. Too often we have heard much comments like, "*Why* do you feel that way?" or "*You shouldn't* feel that way!" It is comments like these subtle forms of rejection that prevent us from being genuine with others.

FEELING WORDS

Once the instructor has internalized these concepts, there are a few exercises that can be used to help students understand the differences between thoughts and feelings and also how to effectively listen and respect how other students feel. Preface these activities with explaining that within the classroom, just like life outside of it, camaraderie and friendship is enhanced when feelings are understood and accepted. Hand out a list of feeling words like these below:

FEELING VOCABULARY

Angry

aggravated
annoyed
defiant
disgusted
enraged
exasperated
frustrated
furious
hateful
hostile
indignant
infuriated
mad
obstinate
outraged
perturbed
peeved
pissed off
rebellious
seething
spiteful
surly
upset
vengeful

Ashamed

apologetic
embarrassed
foolish
guilty
humble
idiotic
mortified
regretful
remorseful
shameful
worthless

Confident

bold
capable
centered

eager
energetic
focused
grounded
hopeful
inspired
keen
optimistic
powerful
productive
strong
sure
trusting

Confused

baffled
befuddled
bewildered
disoriented
flustered
perplexed
puzzled
scattered
troubled
unfocused

Happy

amused
cheerful
delighted
ecstatic
elated
excited
exuberant
gleeful
high
joyful
mischievous

Hurt

abandoned
abused
attacked
belittled
bitter
cheated
disappointed
dismayed
grieving
gypped
humiliated
mournful
sorrowful
rejected
resentful

Loving

affectionate
aroused
caring
devoted
intimate
tender
warm

Sad

despondent
depressed
dismal
low
melancholy
miserable
unhappy
weepy

Satisfied

adequate
content
mellow
peaceful
pleased

Scared

afraid
alarmed
fearful
frightened
horrified
hysterical
insecure
intimidated
nervous
panicky
petrified
terrified
threatened
vulnerable

Surprised

aghast
amazed
astonished
astounded
incredulous
shocked
startled

Thankful

appreciative
grateful
gratified
indebted
obliged
relieved

Thoughtful

challenged
curious
illuminated
informed
interested
pensive
reflective

Uncertain

cynical
doubtful
dubious
distrustful
hesitant
indecisive
pessimistic
skeptical
suspicious
unsure
unsettled

Uncaring

ambivalent
apathetic
bored
busy
detached
exhausted
indifferent
lethargic
lazy
tired

Unmotivated

nonchalant
occupied
selfish
unconcerned

Wanting

empty
envious
homesick
hungry
ignored
jealous
lonely
longing

lustful

Weak

inadequate
burdened
controlled
despairing
discouraged
helpless
hopeless
impotent
inhibited
lost
passive
powerless
restricted
suicidal

Worried

agitated
anxious
bothered
restless
tense
uneasy
unsettled

RIGHT NOW

Each student is to have a blank piece of paper and a pen or a pencil. Then ask this question: "How do you feel right now?" They are to use this form when answering the question: "I feel ________ ." Only one word should follow the word feel. Some examples are: "I feel *tired*," "I feel bored," "I feel *irritated*." Tell them to put a line through the word *feel* and above it write the word *think*. They should easily see the sentence makes no sense. Even have them substitute *feel that* for *feel* and the students will again see that the phrase does not make sense.

THINK THAT

Next have them write, "I feel that this teacher is goofy." Have them line out the word *feel* and above it write *think*. It should now read "I *think* that this teacher is goofy." They will now be able to see that they were not expressing a feeling but rather a thought or an opinion. All the while they could have been feeling confused, frustrated, or irritated—those are feelings. Help them to see the difference and raise their consciousness to how they use and listen to feeling language with their friends.

ACCEPTANCE

When someone chooses to share feelings with us there are various forms of acceptance we can use. Let's say a fellow student says, "Boy that makes me frustrated!" Without even using the word "frustrated," sometimes one can tell by the train of expletives #$!**# and the intensity of voice volume that we think someone is feeling frustrated. Some examples of a proper response to this frustration could be:

"Gee, I don't know if I've ever felt that way before. Can you describe your frustration for me?"

"I can see you look frustrated. What's it like feeling that way?"

"I have felt frustrated before too. I wonder if your frustration is like mine."

BEGIN WITH THE SENSES

In this exercise we want to give students practice describing feelings by using various methods—beginning with the five senses. We will continue to use the "frustrated" feeling as our example. The students, of course, will all have different feelings to describe. First you will read a descriptive question. Following the question is an example of how one could describe the frustrated feeling in response to the question. Once they decide how they are feeling right now they are to write the descriptive question followed by their answer as in the examples below:

1. What color is the feeling? "My frustrated feeling is a dark brown color, sort of like the color of your shoes."
2. What does the feeling smell like? "My frustrated feeling smells dry and musty."
3. What does the feeling taste like? "My frustrated feeling tastes like chewing on old beef jerky or a piece of leather."
4. What does the feeling feel like to the touch? "My frustrated feeling is like rubbing your hand across a rough piece of burlap."
5. What does the feeling sound like? "My frustrated feeling is like the sound of loud static on the radio when I am trying to find a good station."
6. What kind of food best describes this feeling? "My frustrated feeling is like burnt french fries when I want one real bad."
7. Describe this feeling using nature. "My frustrated feeling is like walking through some dry grass that has stickers that pinch me in my socks."
8. What kind of music describes this feeling? "My frustrated feeling is like hard rock with loud twangy guitars. Like the song 'Paradise City' by Guns and Roses."
9. Describe this feeling using sports. "My frustrated feeling is like getting beat so bad that you can't wait for it to be over so you can leave."
10. Paint a picture of this feeling. "My frustrated feeling is the picture of a mother with two or three crying children approaching a long line waiting for a donation of food on a hot day."

PAIR UP

After they have described their feeling in writing for themselves, have each student pair up with the person to their left. Ask each person in turn to share some portions of their ten descriptions with their partner. Then have them reverse roles. Remind all to be good listeners. Some feelings will not lend themselves to all the descriptions above, but there should be a significant number of them represented. Conclude with anyone who wants to share their descriptions of their feelings with the rest of the class.

WATCH THE VIDEO

Now that they have had some experience in describing their feelings, with pen or pencil and paper in hand have them watch a short video clip (one to five minutes) that would serve as a means to stimulating feelings (feel free to find one on YouTube that is appropriate for your class, such as https://www.youtube.com/watch?v=nIsCs9_-LP8). Ask them to write one-word feelings *as they watch*. Their eyes should be on the video as their pen/pencil is writing on the paper. Each student should end up with a set of feeling words written all over the paper. When the video is over have them choose one of the feelings they wrote and describe it in detail. Have them share that with one other person in their group. Then ask volunteers to share their descriptions with the whole class.

KEEPING IN CONTACT

Students keeping in contact with their feelings and able to listen appropriately to other's feelings should not be a one-event experience as they did in these sets of feeling directed activities. Within the context of each week's lessons there should be times to practice the identification, description, and listening to fellow student's feelings. Setting up a regular pattern at the beginning or end of each class period or time of day (it should only take a few minutes) may work best for some classrooms. This small "lesson" will reap great rewards in constructing a positive affective relational tone for the class.

VALUES

Because of the amorality of feelings we teach our students to accept how others feel as a way of expressing our acceptance of who they are as people. But more often than not disagreements occur when there is a conflict between values or the opinions that flow from those values. We live according to our values. Observing how a person lives reveals what they value. Looking through a person's checkbook shows what they value as revealed in how they spend their money. Looking through someone's appointment calendar makes known what they value in how they spend their time. Values are the foundation on which we make our decisions. We develop values from the environment we live in. This environment includes our parents and other family members, neighbors, faith community, media, and our society as a whole. We acquire those values either consciously or unconsciously.

OPINIONS

Opinions are statements we make based on our values. Our opinions may vary in intensity to the degree that we value something. For example if someone values good health it will be actualized in the ways that person eats, exercises, and otherwise treats their body. Someone may also have an opinion that eating red meat is very unhealthy. Their opinion will only be as strong as their willingness to live it out. Everyone is entitled to their opinion.

NEED NOT AGREE

It is just that—a personal statement based on what is valued. We need not agree with another person's values or opinions, but we should respect their right to hold them. Listening to another's "view" is not challenging unless we hear them trying to convince us to accept their opinion as our own. Once we are at peace with our own values and opinions and believe that others have a right to their own we are better able to listen to what they have to say without being threatened.

EXPRESSING OPINIONS

Here is an activity to try with your students. Take a survey of the class on one of the things they value and about which they have an opinion. One that seems to draw much approval is music. In today's culture you could also use sport teams, singers, TV programs, or other media. Many students value good music and have strongly held opinions about some aspects of it. They live it out by listening to a lot of it.

ARGUING

First ask them to yell out the best music-playing radio station in their locality. Often it becomes a shouting match with each student trying to outdo the others, sometimes while trying to disparage others in their choice of stations. If music is not a high value to your students, you can use the same strategy with either sport teams, singers, TV programs, or the like. The whole point is for the class to hear students arguing about each other's opinions on one specific area.

LISTENING TO ANOTHER'S OPINION

Now have them pair up (forming a dyad) with someone of a differing opinion of whatever topic was chosen. One person from each dyad must now explain to the other the reasons behind his/her opinion. The listening person in the dyad shall not interrupt. The listener should take on the attitude of being interested in the other's opinion. *Accepting* what the other person is saying does not mean that they are *agreeing* with them but just curious by how that opinion was formulated. Throughout this process the listener should:

- be attentive
- be aware of the other's emotions
- comment on times they may have felt similarly
- maintain good eye contact
- respect the right of the other to have a differing opinion
- use physical acceptance gestures like nodding
- ask questions
- put themselves in the other's shoes
- checking for understanding: Wherever possible say to the other something like "What I hear you saying is . . . am I correct?" Repeat until what you interpret they are saying is corroborated by their affirmative responses.

EXTENSION

This process is to be repeated with the listener now sharing the reasons for his/her opinion with the other in the dyad now becoming the listener. This is then followed up with a general class discussion about what was learned in the process of expressing and listening to another's opinion. Let them know that throughout the fabric of this year they will be working with other students who will have different opinions of various class topics and activities. Being able to work effectively with others will be most beneficial in their learning, as well as preparing them to extend their developing listening skills to family, friends, and future co-workers.

LISTENING SKILLS

While this component can be placed in any suitable position in your course, it is suggested that its components be reviewed whenever new groups or teams are formed. The key issue here is that every student wants to be listened to and each has something useful to offer. Even the wrong answer calls forth critical thinking skills on the part of the others in the group to recognize what's wrong and then help their fellow students to the correct understanding.

HEARING OR LISTENING?

Hearing is not the same as listening. Hearing is a passive physiological experience produced by any sound entering the ears. Listening is an active process of the person being open and able to accept what another student has to say without necessarily agreeing. A good listener can respond in ways that inform the speaker that her/his comments are valuable

ROLE PLAY

It's fun at this juncture for each group to put on a little role play. Three groups of four will prepare three skits. The first group's skit will show two students not listening to each other. The second group's skit will depict one student listening and the other not. The third skit will portray two students actively listening. Each of the other groups are to develop a set of criteria that tells a person when they are listening and when they are being listened to. Many of the concepts from *Thoughts* vs. *Feelings* as well as *Values* and *Opinions* will be helpful. Following the presentation of the skits to the whole class, discuss some ways that an individual can call the attention of others on their team when they believe that they are being listened to and when not.

BODY LANGUAGE

If none of the groups have mentioned the way one positions his/her body when listening, call for some of the ways that indicate a person is listening by how they carry themselves (leaning toward or away from the speaker, location of hands and arms, positioning of head, facial gestures and focus of eyes). Make note that while in the Western culture it is considered a positive sign when someone "looks you in the eye," in some cultures this is deemed inappropriate for ordinary conversation. Call for volunteers to role play the various positive and negative ways of listening with your body.

CHECKING FOR UNDERSTANDING

Checking for understanding is perhaps one of the best methods students should use in any listening situation. The basic idea here is that more often than not we do not understand the full meaning of what a speaker is trying to communicate to us. So in order to find out if one student has the correct interpretation of what another has shared he/she could politely stop the speaker at appropriate intervals and say "Now, what I understood you to say was_________________."

ON TRACK?

"Am I on track? Where am I confused? Where did I miss your meaning?" Notice that these are all "I" messages. They do not assume that the speaker erred in his/her comments but rather that "I" did not receive what the speaker intended. It is courteous and presumes good intentions on the part of the speaker.

PRACTICE CLARIFICATION

If the speaking student wishes to check for understanding he/she could ask one of those listening, "I want to make sure that I was clear in my comment to you just now. Would you please help me out and tell me what you understood me to say?" Again, the burden of responsibility is on the one who wishes to check for understanding. It presumes that the listener is positively connected in the conversation.

PAIR UP

Because this is not a normal part of our everyday talk, it would again be a good idea to practice clarification by pairing the students up and having one be the listener and the other the speaker. Have the speakers explain to the listeners something that they are good at, for example, cooking a particular dish, playing a musical instrument, performing some sport activity or dance, etc. Have them then change roles and repeat the process. Ask them how a student would rephrase the check-for-understanding questions to better fit into their modes of conversation. This clarification technique would be very valuable during ordinary classroom discussions.

DEALING WITH MISTAKES

This concept is most critical in dealing with the many ways we "goof up" as we go through life. As students work in groups, the ways in which they deal with their own and others' mistakes can go a long way in making their daily experience in the classroom a positive one. The central aspect of Forgiving Learning is to develop a classroom culture where mistakes, errors, and the like are seen as a normal part of the human condition. It is how students and teacher *respond* to mistakes in the personal, relational, and instructional arenas that sets the tone for learning. Once again remember that the brain's limbic system is always assessing the feeling tone of the environment and is the gateway to the neocortex, where learning takes place.

CRITICAL SELF/OTHER TALK

In this exercise the students will examine how they talk to themselves and others when a mistake occurs. Again, have them sit in groups of four. Each student is to have a pen/pencil and a piece of paper. First they are to make a list of comments they frequently make to themselves when they mess up. Exclamations such as, "Duh!," "My bad," and expletives that may include cuss words are common. There is a need to be flexible here. Even though the common decorum of the class should not support some of this language, the truth is that some students do speak to themselves in this fashion. For the sake of enhancing student self-worth, it should be tolerated in this activity.

EXTRACTING MEANING

Student are to respond out loud what they wrote and have a group secretary then write them down including duplicates only once. While taking turns, each student is to comment on another student's negative self-talk. The comments should include what they think is the message behind the self-critical statements of another and whether or not the remark is healthy for that student's self-worth. Why or why not? How do they think a fellow student is affected by a regular diet of self-criticism? An important point to make is that often students treat themselves and others the way they have been treated in the past when they have made a mistake.

POSITIVE SELF-TALK

Now the students in the group are to brainstorm some self-directed positive comments that could have been made. This positive self-talk should acknowledge the mistake, but in addition now encourage the students to forgive themselves for the faux pas and give them hope for the next opportunity. Each student should write these down. An example would be for a basketball player who just missed a shot: "I was way off on that one. With a little more practice I will improve."

ANOTHER'S GOOF

Students know well what types of responses they normally have when another student goofs up. Examples include perhaps the wrong answer to a question the teacher asks in class, dropping an ice cream cone, or making an inappropriate comment to another student. Comments such as, "lame," "yea . . . right," "okayyyyyy!" or even the rolling of one's eyes at the failings of another are all forms of put downs. Instead, there are supportive things one can say when another student errs, "That's okay, you will get it the next time." "Don't worry about it, I make mistakes all the time."

COMICS

Most students have read the comics. With two pieces of 8 1/2" x 11" paper, each student is to make two three-to-five cartoon panels (one for negative self-talk, the second for negative other-talk) using stick figures and comments. One panel should show a person making a mistake of some kind and then some positive self-talk they could use. The second panel will show a person making a mistake with someone else saying some positive other-talk.

FUNNY

The funnier the better: "Oh, darn, I missed getting that hot oatmeal in my mouth. I will get better when I use a spoon rather than my hands." After you are done with this exercise post some of the better cartoons on the bulletin board. They will serve as a good reminder of how to positively deal with mistakes. This will be particularly helpful when they are given the opportunity to rework assignments and/or return for another try at classroom assessments.

AFFIRMATION

This is a good closing experience to all the activities designed to help set the relational tone of the class. So often students just respond to the goof ups in life and forget that they need to hear that they are good people who have good qualities and are capable of doing good things. Students really love to hear affirmations about themselves. Students can be reminded that this is one reason that yearbook signing at the end of the school year is so important to them.

NICE THINGS

Students can't wait to read what nice things their classmates have to say about them. Make a list of everyone in the class for each student and pass it out. Tell each student to circle their own name on their student list copy. The coach includes his/her name there also. Collect each of these class lists, each with one circled name, and randomly distribute them on desks around the room. (Everyone likes to hear nice things said about themselves—teachers included.)

MILLING AROUND

Tell each student to circle his/her name. Collect the lists and place them randomly around the room. If possible play some quiet background music. Once given the prompt to start, students are to mill around the room writing complimentary comments and signing their names to each one. One could read, "Hi, Bob, I don't really know you that well but you seem to be kind and a good listener. Cheryl Smith." If a student does not know someone well enough to write a positive quality, he/she should go up and ask that person to tell them something about themselves. This really helps the students to get to know each other. If all goes well each student and coach will have the list with their name circled and comments from all the other students. Ask students to keep these in a safe place so that when they're down they can reread these to help them see the good they possess.

FOUR

Working with Teams

WHY USE TEAMS?

Human beings are social animals. They live and work in communities of people. Upbringing is in small groups—families, classrooms, gangs—and people learn early to be comfortable in small groups. This helps them to develop commitment to a team, which they might not have to a large organisation. Ask people whom they work for and they'll give the company name. Ask them what they see in their mind's eye, and the chances are it will be their immediate manager and/or colleagues. People can lose sight of the big picture, especially in large organizations. It is their work "family" to whom they relate.

This social cohesion gives us strength. Many tasks are beyond individual human beings. Growth and development comes through interaction within groups, as does the completion of any major task. Groups also offer continuity. A group can continue work on a task when individuals leave or take a break.

This cohesion and continuity mean that well organised groups—teams—can improve productivity in the organizations in which they work by between eight and eleven per cent. Teams can also contribute to the improvement of the working climate, because of the improved relationships that they should engender between employees.[1]

PREPARATION

We are preparing our students for living in the world—whether the world of work, service, or some other interactive venture. The fact is that unless students choose to sequester themselves in some solitary endeavor, the vast majority will be collaborating with other human beings on a regular basis. The classroom provides a unique atmosphere for socialization. Students left to their own devices will most often mingle only with those with whom they are comfortable.

BARRIERS

Stereotypes, prejudice, and hearsay often create the strongest barriers to a collegial learning atmosphere. Fear and mistrust are the key blocks that need to be reduced to help bring our students into the mainstream of our multicultural society. Their ability to offer their intellectual skills to their immediate environment and to humanity as a whole is critically dependent on their willingness to contribute and communicate to all types of people, including those with whom they are comfortable and those with whom they are not.

SHARE RESPONSIBILITY

Teaming breaks the isolation of students thinking that they are the only ones who do or do not understand a given concept. As students share responsibility for understanding and decision making, they will develop techniques to determine if other students in the group have understood what they are communicating. Forgiving Learning will thrive when all classroom students share in the culture of learning from their mistakes and the persistence of returning again and again to address their weaknesses.

MAIN STRUCTURE

Teaming deepens the understanding and communication among students and teacher because you are not just talking about subject matter but relational skills as well. Teams are the main structure that paves the way to a relational classroom where the limbic system (old mammalian brain) senses a positive atmosphere and becomes the segue to preparing the neocortex for learning.

SCAFFOLDING

Many students are often of the mind that they are engaging in "school-type" learning all alone. Good classroom pedagogy provides some type of inter-student scaffolding where students are led to help each other along in the learning endeavor. An instructor will invariably provide some form of content-focused explanation that many students just don't get. But if the teacher can find one or more students from a team who do understand, those students can "translate" teacher lingo into student-comprehensible language that others do connect with. Inter-student camaraderie on a team can foster personal association with that group.

TEAM SELECTION

It is suggested that groupings/teams be three to four students each. Begin by creating arbitrary team assignments. One suggestion for teams of four each is for students in the class count off 1, 2, 3, 4 and repeat this sequence up to the number of *teams* you wish to have in the class—assuming that the number of students in the class is evenly divisible by 4. Then have those with like numbers group themselves together (all the 1s would be a team, and likewise for 2s, 3s, and 4s). You may have to have some teams of three and/or five to make it come out correctly. Arbitrariness is important here because in the world when working and interacting with others, individuals often do not have a say regarding with whom they will be interacting.

RESTRUCTURING

Teams can be changed every quarter or so. Once the home teams have been established, going through the Myers-Briggs with students can provide a unique way of getting to know each other and how they can best work in a group. When at some later date you choose to restructure the groups (perhaps by putting a more skilled student in each group), you can always use the Myers-Briggs as a jumping off point in appreciating each other's learning style.

WHY MYERS-BRIGGS?

Forgiving Learning was developed to cooperate and enhance what the neocortex portion of the human brain is already designed to do: create and use programs. We call this learning. Accessing and enhancing the engagement of the neocortex is the work of the old mammalian portion of the brain that we call the limbic system. This portion of the brain operates best when the relational atmosphere of its environment is positive.

HARMONY

It is not enough to just have students "working together" in teams. In order for the "working together" criteria to be effective, the harmony within each student and among students needs to be nurtured. This is the purpose of understanding and appreciating both one's own and other student's learning styles. Using the Myers-Briggs concepts is a way of facilitating this.

TEACHING STYLE

Before doing this, however, it is recommended that the instructor who is not familiar with the Myers-Briggs and its use with his/her teaching style take a few moments to take the online version at http://www.16personalities.com/free-personality-test. While there are many workshops across the United States (see http://www.myersbriggs.org/using-type-as-a-professional/certify-to-administer-the-mbti-tool/), sufficient understanding of the concepts and how they apply to teachers is important (see http://www.myersbriggs.org/type-use-for-everyday-life/type-and-learning/ and http://www.personalitypathways.com/MBTI_articles4.html). The Myers-Briggs basics were presented in chapter 2. The more teachers understand and appreciate their own teaching styles, the more they will value the importance of their students' learning styles in the classroom and beyond.

STARTING POINT

Like their teachers, students need a starting point in determining their Myers-Briggs learning style. Initially the short form of the Myers-Briggs sorter, which was used as qualification to purchase it, required appropriate training. But now there are Myers-Briggs online versions that are for free. And because many students have "tablets," they can access and use them to get an initial reading of their learning preferences.

YOUNG STUDENTS

It is important to note that the Myers-Briggs preferences and functions (I, E, S, N, T, F, J, P) may not be sufficiently differentiated at a young age. This means that young students may not have matured enough for them to become aware of how they make decisions in their life. As a rule of thumb, it is recommend that the following online Myers-Briggs sorter be used beginning with middle school (approximately twelve- to thirteen-year-old) children (http://www.16personalities.com/free-personality-test).

BETTER FIT

This online version should take no more than ten to fifteen minutes. In the next step students should write down their four letters, for example,

ISTJ. Then they should read their type description at http://www.16personalities.com/personality-types and ask themselves if it rings true to how they see themselves. If not, students should then re-examine the letters as reported by the sorter and see if they are on the borderline in any of the preferences. For example, if the sorter says that their style is best represented as an ISTJ but the choice between S and N is close, read the INTJ and see if that is a better fit, and so forth for any of the other letters.

BEST FIT

If a student has a friend in the class who knows them well, they can ask for that student's input. "Which best describes me?" It may be possible for students to take their profile home and get parent input as well. Although this is not strictly speaking a psychological *test* (it is a *sorter*—there are no right or wrong answers), the school site or district may have some guidelines about parent permission. The focus here should be that the Myers-Briggs sorter and resulting *best fit* "learning style" and students' interpretation can be of great benefit to them in their schooling and beyond.

CHOICE

The best fit learning style is what the student decides after sufficient explanation (see chapter 2) of what each letter means and input from the Myers-Briggs sorter, related descriptions, and perhaps family and friends. It is important to remember that every student has all preference and functions (I, E, S, N, T, F, J, P) operating on some level. The best fit simply means that each student has an inclination or favorite way of operating. This is the choice they make.

TEAM INTRODUCTIONS

Once the coach has determined who is on each home team, they are to meet together, each student bringing along with them a 3" x 5" card with their "best fit" four letters written on it in large caps. All of the students on the team are to introduce themselves with their names as well as a description of their learning styles, either in their own words or using the description from the website http://www.16personalities.com/personality-types.

DISCUSSION

They then begin a discussion on what could be their potential strengths and weaknesses as a team. They will go through the descriptions of each of the preferences and functions *as they apply to individuals working within a team.* One member can read each paragraph and the conversation can address the question, "How does this apply to us?"

SENSING TYPE TEAM MEMBERS

All students need to take in information before making a decision. There are two ways students prefer to get that information: either through the five senses (S) or through their intuition (N). When working with sensates on a team, all members should know that sensates make up approximately 75 percent of the population. They are the "Joe Fridays" (from Dragnet) of the group, "Just the facts, Ma'am." They want the "specifics" and the details when addressing a problem, a lot like Sherlock Holmes. They are earth bound, grounded in the reality of here and now. They like concrete visible examples of what they are to learn. They like simplicity without a lot of fluff.

IMPLEMENTATION

Sensates are not good at brainstorming. They have hunches, but often ignore them as they view them as too nebulous and not anchored in reality. Sensates like step-by-step procedures and prefer to follow well-established routines rather than breaking new ground. They plod along in getting things done, seldom making factual errors and tending to be good at precise work. If the team has a task to complete they would be good at establishing a linear sequence of time and actions. Sensates are good at implementing a plan.

INTUITIVE TYPE TEAM MEMBERS

Intuitive (N) types gather information differently than sensates. They make up about 25 percent of students. If you hold an apple in front of a sensate he or she might say, "There is a bright red apple." An intuitive might say, "Hey, that reminds me of apple pie or apple sauce." They go beyond what the eye sees to possibilities and associations. Intuitive types make the mind tell the eyes what it sees. They are the "idea" people in a brainstorming session, dreaming and imagining potential solutions. They do not want to be limited by the facts, but rather by what is possible. They are not bound to what "is."

HUNCHES

When reading, intuitives go behind the words to other connections and implications. They work in bursts of energy rather than in a step-by-step fashion. As for some detectives (Columbo, for example), hunches are a key aspect in gathering critical insights. Intuitive types are future oriented, not anchored in the present moment, so they tend to be more "flighty" than their sensate teammates.

SENSATES HELPED BY INTUITIVES

When working on a common project or specific assigned task, sensing types need input from intuitives and likewise intuitives need sensates. Thus when there is a team that has all sensate types, someone must play the role of an intuitive. During the team discussions the intuitives will often be the spark that brings in new ideas and looks far ahead to implications of a given path. It is important within the team dynamic to allow the intuitives to complete their ideas before bringing them back to earth with questions of facts and details.

EXAMPLE

Here is an example of a possible conversation within a group that is trying to plan a school dance. The intuitive says, "Yeah, we can have a live band and pizza and punch for everyone." Now a sensate chimes in and says, "But how are we going to pay for the band and buy the pizza?" In this approach an intuitive could experience his/her idea squashed by the detail questions posed by the sensate. A better way for the sensate to respond to the intuitive's *idea* would be to say, "That's a great proposal, now what suggestions do you have about how to finance it?" This response will effectively tap into the intuitive's skill in again coming up with a creative funding plan and could also result in the sensate's desire for facts and details.

INTUITIVES HELPED BY SENSATES

In a similar fashion intuitives on a team need the skills of a sensate when making a decision. If there are no sensates on the team then an intuitive team member should act as one searching for additional information. Sensates can better manage time and resources to the completion of a task. They can examine the details of the endeavor and keep track of what needs to be accomplished. Intuitives should question sensates about whether or not the team is on task and if they have addressed any details.

MUTUAL RESPECT

Sensates will keep the pace of the work manageable rather than operating in fits and spurts as intuitives are wont to do. They should take the ideas and inspirations of the intuitives and make them doable rather than just pie in the sky. Sensates need to fight the tendency to see intuitives as flighty and impractical. Intuitives likewise need to resist implying that sensates are plodding and picky. Each needs to respect the preferences of the other and value the gifts they bring to the team.

THINKING AND FEELING IN TEAMS

Once the team has gathered all the information it needs both through the sensing and intuitive members, it is time to make a decision. Students have two different methods of coming to a decision: either through analytical logic (called thinking types, T) or relational logic (called feeling types, F). Thinking types make up approximately 50 percent of the population. In Western culture, 60 percent of those are male and 40 percent are female. While feeling types also make up 50 percent of the population, 40 percent are male and 60 percent are female.

DECISIONS

Thinking types prefer to make decisions objectively and impersonally. Feeling types prefer decisions considering personal situations subjectively. When working on a team, T types do not need harmony among members to function well but F types do. Thinking types often behave critically and may show little concern for the feelings of others. Feeling types are much more sensitive to the relational tone of the team and unlike their T teammates do not participate well in team activities if there is conflict within the team. F types want to make decisions that everyone likes. T types are more concerned that the decision is correct regardless of how it affects others.

THINKING HELPED BY FEELING

While T types relate best to other T types (where their talk has a clear beginning, middle, and end) they need the feeling type's sensitivity to the personal nature of the communication to ameliorate hurting another's feelings without knowing it. Feeling types on a team can serve it best in establishing a tone of understanding and acceptance. In Forgiving Learning, where the focus is on reconciling one's errors and learning from them, F types can bring a spirit of toleration when mistakes are made by teammates.

BENEFITS

Feeling types are good at distributing praise and positive enthusiasm for whatever tasks are at hand. Whatever path the team chooses to take, the feeling type can take the impersonal logic of a T type and show how others could benefit from it without necessarily agreeing with it: T type says, "If we want to finish this project, then we should all stay after school to complete it." F type says, "Even though some of us may not want to stay after school, we could have a good time together and get it done with some fun, too."

FEELING HELPED BY THINKING

Feeling types may get so involved with the tone of the team that they minimize the need to organize its activities and logically analyze the information to the completion of a task, which are strengths of thinking types. Keeping the team working toward a goal without being bogged down by how others may feel is another attribute thinking types bring to team endeavors. They can maintain some degree of personal impartiality when arriving at a decision and can assure that everyone is treated fairly.

ACCOUNTABLE

Thinking types can operate well without the need for praise. They are good at detecting flaws in ideas and have the energy to be firm with logical processes without letting personal preferences rule the day. Thinking types will hold the team accountable to policies and rules that govern their activities, "Well, we can't do that because it goes against the guidelines we were given."

INTROVERSION AND EXTROVERSION WITHIN TEAMS

The dynamics of introverts (I) and extroverts (E) within teams is perhaps the most interesting and obvious of the preferences. Extroverts make up approximately 75 percent of all students and introverts make up 25 percent. Making decisions on a team takes time and energy. Introverts go inside themselves to find that energy, much like the power to run a laptop comes from the internal battery. They appear more quiet and introspective.

PROCESSING TIME

An extrovert is rather like a desktop computer that has to be plugged into the wall to get its energy. They prefer to make their decisions by some activity like hearing themselves talk (or write) and have quicker processing times. Asking a classroom question will determine who the extroverts are by how quickly they will raise their hands. For introverts it takes more time to reflect and come to a resolution of any issue so they will want a slower pace in team operation. For the team to get an introverted teammate's input, someone must directly ask them. More often than not, they will just answer what they were asked and not add any elaboration.

INTROVERTS WITHIN A TEAM

Introverts usually have fewer friends than extroverts, but their friendships go deeper. They are better equipped to handle long projects than extroverts. Introverts operate better with some degree of quiet so that they can concentrate. They do not like interruptions with their work and will usually wait to speak rather than volunteer their ideas. With less eye contact, they sometimes appear to be aloof and apart, but are actually more often mentally engaged in their thoughts and feelings. Introverts can be misjudged as "loners" in a derogatory fashion, as if something is wrong with them. They may be often classified as "persons of few words," but when they do volunteer to share, their ideas are deep and well thought out. They can bring more reflective and peaceful processes to team activities and discussions.

EXTROVERTS WITHIN A TEAM

Extroverts bring a load of energy to a team. They are natural cheerleaders. Extroverts relish participating in activities and talking. They easily share their possessions, thoughts, and feelings. They are often the source of laughter and noise during team engagement. Extroverts are good communicators. They do their best thinking as they listen to *themselves* give answers and explanations.

GO WITH FLOW

They easily make friends and usually have many of them, although the friendships may be somewhat superficial. Extroverts easily volunteer for activities but operate much better in short projects for which energy does not have to be sustained over a long time. They do not mind interruptions and are usually more than willing to "go with the flow," although they can become impatient if things go too slowly.

INTROVERTS HELPED BY EXTROVERTS

Extroverts can help introverts become better teammates by actively including them in discussions, asking them questions, and inviting their participation in all activities. Introverts are helped by extroverts when the introverts' contributions are valued and offers of friendship are extended to them. Extroverts who normally manage the energy level of the team can include times of silence for individual thought and reduce the number of interruptions to team conversations and actions. Extroverts can suggest a "count to ten" mechanism before answering comments to give the introvert time to reflect before responding.

EXTROVERTS HELPED BY INTROVERTS

Introverts, for their part, can help extroverts by participating with team activities rather than remaining passive and reclusive. Some team activities could begin with a few quiet moments for all to stop and think before doing anything. This will slow the extroverted quick decisions preference. Introverts can initiate some "one-on-one" dyad discussions before opening it up for everyone to share. Breaking the team into "twos" will help the extrovert to experience the value of deeper and quieter dialogue rather than the more common free-for-all conversations. This would focus on the extrovert experiencing the preferences of the introvert.

JUDGING AND PERCEPTIVE TYPE STUDENTS

Although the entire Myers-Briggs sorter and resulting descriptions of preferences is based on the work of Jung, there was no mention in his writings of the Judging (J) and Perceiving (P) functions. They were inferred from his work by Katherine Briggs and her daughter Isabel Myers. These overarching functions describe a student's orientation to life. Either they prefer a structure-oriented life that wants to make decisions, judging (J), or they want their environments flowing and tentative, perceptive (P). Students are split 50 percent for J and P.

TEAM DYNAMICS

This is a critical function for team operation. If the team does not understand what drives its work, there will be conflicting purposes. The fact is that both J and P type students make great contributions to team dynamics. When is it important to engage the team in the *overarching gathering of information function (P)* using the sensate (S) and intuitive (N) preferences? When is it important to engage the team in the *overarching making a decision function (J)* using the thinking (T) analytical logic and feeling (F) relational logic preferences?

JUDGING TYPES WITHIN A TEAM

The difference is simple. The judging (J) type student lives an organized and structured life. They like making decisions (T/F) and usually do so with conviction and confidence. They will bring to the team a drive to have its actions organized to the completion of a goal or task. They will desire to control and regulate team plans and schedules. Judging types may tend to be abrupt as they want the team to finish its activities in good order. If a deadline is decided by either the team or the teacher, they will often be tense until it is done. Their personal assignments may not be of the highest quality because their main focus is getting it done and they are less concerned with the quality of their work. Judging types will most often get their assignments in on time or even early.

PERCEPTIVE TYPES WITHIN A TEAM

Perceptive (P) type students live flexible lives continuing to take in information (S/N) with all decisions remaining tentative and unsure. Perceptive students can work on many projects at once yet have difficulty completing any of them. Their work on a team will strive for quality rather than completion. They will be curious and open minded and will easily move from one activity to another.

RELAXED

Perceptives will probe by asking good questions and easily handle glitches in a team's progress by adapting alternate routes to the process. They will have trouble sticking to a schedule and will need flexibility to be included in the team's plans. Their tendency to postpone does not mean that they are lazy but rather that they want to spend more time investigating and taking in information. They are often relaxed and laid back without a sense of urgency. They are usually calm during the process of a task and will usually get tense just before it becomes due.

JUDGING TYPES CAN HELP PERCEIVING TYPES

Although it is common for Js to see P's need for flexibility as a sign of chaos, they can help Ps by breaking tasks down into smaller pieces that can be more easily completed. As situations often change, Js can call on Ps to find new ways of adapting rather than rushing to a conclusion. Js need to develop patience in working with Ps, recognizing their contribution to the team is to ensure the quality of their work. They can give Ps reminders of when assignments and projects are due and encourage them to slowly bring their contributions to closure. "Do you have any idea when you will be done?" Js preparing a schedule of what needs to be completed and when will help Ps move along in their contributions.

PERCEPTIVE TYPES CAN HELP JUDGING TYPES

Perceptive types can frequently see judging type's need for structure and organization as authoritarian. They can begin to appreciate the role of Js on a team if they ask themselves the question, "If Js don't organize this, who will?" Knowing that Js can sometimes rush to decisions without enough information, they can pose questions along the way that the Js may not have considered. This will slow the process down so that a conclusion may be more valid.

FLEXIBILITY

Judging types may not notice new things that need to be done. Ps can bring those items to J's attention so that they can be dealt with in a timely manner. Js can more easily have the flexibility to let go of plans if they get permission from other team members. Ps can lead this effort when it seems to be of benefit to the current endeavor. This Myers-Briggs information and insight into the contribution of individual students to teamwork should permeate the functioning of the class. It will also go a long way in enabling students to better relate to other students and teachers in other classes and outside of school.

TEAM NAME

Identifying oneself as a member of a team that is designed to be a support network for its members is a student-friendly activity. In the Forgiving Learning process there are two types of teams with which a student is to be associated. The first is their home team. This is the first team with whom they went through all the introductory activities. They will meet with their home team once each week during inter-team academic *challenges* (described below).

FUN

As a fun formation activity, each home team is to construct a banner with a chosen team name, such as, "The wild chickens," "Perplexed," etc. All students are to have input as to the name and coloring and design of the banner. Large pieces of colored construction paper along with glue, tape, colored markers, pens, pencils, scissors, and the like are to be provided. All the banners are to be posted around the classroom. The team is then to select a team captain or spokesperson. The team captain's responsibility is to facilitate the team in arriving at a consensus response to the academic challenges.

ACADEMIC TEAM

During the course of the school year, students are to be assigned to a second team called the academic team. The constituency of the academic teams are changed every six weeks or so. The academic team is the one students work with during the various daily academic activities. If a student is always with the same people his/her role can become stagnant. They are often stereotyped and choose to continue to behave in a particular fashion because they believe others expect it of them.

WELCOME

Teaming gives students a chance to make people and their ideas feel welcome. This is because they must become mutually dependent and practice consensus decision making. They have the opportunity to practice introductions, compliments, and treating others with respect. It also refreshes the classroom atmosphere when groupings are changed at determined intervals. Academic teaming also helps students believe that they are not alone in the classroom learning process.

THE AFFIRMER

After each academic team has been constituted and worked together for a week or so, then every student in the class has the opportunity to nominate what is called the *affirmer* for the week (usually on Monday for the previous week). Students can nominate someone from either their home or academic team as affirmer for the past week. They must verbally share what that student did, for example, "Paul listened well to how I was feeling," "Mary really helped our team finish the lab," etc. These names are put on small slips of paper and placed in a bowl. The one that is drawn out gets a special prize at the teacher's discretion. (Be creative here. One example is a "free assignment" coupon.) This keeps the idea of being a positive influence on your team alive.

CONTENT CHALLENGES

Once each week students meet with their home teams. During this time the instructor poses a subject matter content question to all the classroom home teams. They are to discuss the question and come to a consensus answer. Consensus here means that each member of the team can "live with" a mutually agreed upon response.

NO LOSING

The teacher then goes to each team and listens to the captain articulate their team's answer, verbally or in writing. If it is correct then a classroom commissioner (selected by the whole class for the year) is to record a *win* on a prepared bulletin board chart where wins are recorded. In this way all teams have the possibility of acquiring a *win*. There is no losing. These same questions could be precursors to questions that will be asked of the team during mastery assessment conferences (described in chapter 5).

FORGIVEN ANSWERS

Those teams who don't win the weekly content question can reconstitute their answer by pointing out their errors in thinking and how they could rectify it. Their first incorrect answer would then be forgiven. They could all come in together at some mutually agreed upon time (at lunch or after school, etc.). This builds persistence and focuses on learning from one's failures. If every home team has at least one win then the entire class will get a certain prize, and if each home team has two wins then a more valuable prize will be given. Rewards such as "free assignment coupons" are up to the teacher's discretion. The whole point is to have rewards in support of a collective classroom effort.

MY BRAIN IS FULL

In Forgiving Learning the coach prepares each day's lesson so that there is a feedback mechanism to assure that the experience of each new concept is at the appropriate rate for satisfactory student comprehension. When students realize that they are approaching a limit in their understanding, they must be encouraged to so inform their instructor before the input activity/discussion goes any further. A simple student comment like, "My brain is full" or an agreed upon action, like waving a piece of paper in the air would be signal enough for more time to digest and process the input.

CHECK WITH NEIGHBOR

Another such feedback mechanism is one called "check with your neighbor." Have one student explain to another on their team the central concept of the lesson. Each student in turn responds with his/her understanding within each team, and so forth for the others. The coach can check with a "reporter" from each team as well as individual members to see if the team has an appropriate level of comprehension.

TEAM EVALUATIONS

From time to time when teams have been together for at least two weeks it would be healthy for the members of the group to evaluate its team interactions. Make sure that this is *not a free for all* but instead focused on specific group skills. Delineate the skills by creating a response form that they can use as a jumping off point for their discussion, for example, "Did you carefully listen? Did you experience being listened to?" "Were you able to give compliments?" "Accept compliments?" "Listen to others' feelings, thoughts and opinions?" "Deal with your and others' mistakes?" "Come to consensus on team decisions?" Wherever one or more students express an area of dissatisfaction, encourage a constructive conversation between members to rectify and enhance the intra-team communication.

EXPECTED RESULTS

If the teaming structure has been successful there should be a number of expected results. It should be found that students will show progress in communication and listening skills. Each student should become familiar with others in the class. Students should demonstrate an improved ability to think and solve problems in a group setting as well as exhibiting confidence in dealing with new concepts.

CONTRIBUTE POSITIVELY

With the neocortex operating at a high level, students should exhibit an ability to not only grasp course content, but also become actively and hopefully enthusiastically engaged in the learning endeavor. And as a long-term goal, students should be able to move into a new group of people, be presented with a new situation, and be able to intellectually contribute positively with them.

NOTE

1. Shell Live Wire at http://www.shell-livewire.org/business-library/employing-people/managing-teams/why-use-teams/.

FIVE

Introducing Forgiving Learning in the Classroom

Every grade level, course, and cadre of students is different from any other. It is the professional instructor in the classroom who can best determine the timing, intensity, and modifications necessary to make Forgiving Learning adaptable to their students while keeping its major tenets intact. Repeated here for emphasis those tenets are:

- The teacher taking on the mindset of a coach. Enthusiasm for students and topics studied are key elements.
- Teaming reduces anxiety by changing the relationship with fellow students from that of competitors to that of a cooperative sense of camaraderie.
- The learning experience must be designed to maximize student comprehension, not to prepare for external high-stakes testing.
- Content is to be made relevant and meaningful to students.
- Praise, constructive criticism, and suggestions for improvement must constitute the basis for every response to a student's work and assessment.
- Written and/or oral comments must replace scores and grades on all student work.
- Mistakes are a part of the learning process. Accepting errors without punishment must become a common practice in all that students do.
- Requiring that 100 percent of assignments be done with unlimited resubmissions until quality has been achieved is a viable goal.
- Some form of student-teacher mastery conferences, demonstrations, presentations, and the like, which provide multiple sources of

evidence of what students know and are able to do is both a valid and a satisfying experience for students and teachers.
- The ability to revisit weaknesses discovered in assignments and during the mastery conferences give the student the sense that forgiveness is real and progress is more important than grades and scores.
- Forgiving Learning must be used as a key component of any grading process, which includes a meeting with students and their self-evaluation.

SUGGESTED SEQUENCE

What follows is a suggested sequence of events, concepts, or actions that could be used to introduce all the ideas behind Forgiving Learning to students. It is the professional in the classroom who is responsible for adjusting and modifying this suggested sequence to best fit his/her student clientele. Depending on the class, this initial process could take two to three weeks. The length of time to spend on each of these elements is up to the instructor's discretion. They will each be addressed within this chapter in succession as they appear below. The heading of each will be indicated in *italics*. Following each heading will be the key aspect of each topic that was presented in detail in earlier chapters.

- Teacher being a coach
- Classroom teams and teammates
- Banner, captain, commissioner
- Written comments
- Mistakes forgiven if readdressed
- Portfolio of work
- Challenge questions
- Mastery conferences
- Grades
- Lessons of the Karate Kid
- Stereotypes
- Negative criticism
- Thoughts vs. feelings
- Opinions vs. values
- Hearing vs. listening in conversations
- Dealing with mistakes
- Affirming self and others
- Myers-Briggs

TRANSITIONS

Although most of these have been addressed in chapters 1 through 4, additional commentary will be given in order to make the transition from concept to application more seamless.

TEACHER BEING A COACH

Most students enter a classroom with ideas of what a teacher is, how teachers are to behave, and what their relationships with students should be like. Teachers introducing themselves as their "coach" will be a surprise if not a shock for many of them. How the teacher does this should be consistent with their personality and comfort zone. Calling out students' names during the first roll call of the year is a type of introduction. Teachers asking their students to call them "coach" is likewise an introduction, but also challenging. As students begin to understand where the concept of coaching comes from and why their instructor has taken on that model, its use will become more comfortable and meaningful. (See chapters 1 and 2.)

CLASSROOM TEAMS AND TEAMMATES

Coaching and teams go hand in hand. The structure that all students are to be working in teams should be an easy sell. More than likely students have worked with others in groups or cadres of one sort or another. The focus here should be on the camaraderie and mutual support others can bring to each member of the team. Individual students are no longer alone in this classroom learning experience and do not have to *compete* with others, but rather *cooperate* with them. Once students are made aware of how learning is a major function of their brain, they can appreciate the way being collegial can bring a sense of harmony to the old mammalian brain and therefore can make their neocortexes operate at a higher level. (See chapters 1, 2, and 4.)

BANNER, CAPTAIN, COMMISSIONER

The reality of a home team will become evident when they work together to come up with a team name and make an appropriate banner to post in the classroom. Deciding on a name and making a banner is a nonthreatening way for students to get to know each other and have fun at the same time. Selecting a team captain gives that student responsibility for actually reporting consensus answers during the challenge questioning (see below) and to manage team activities and decision making. The classroom commissioner is the one who organizes the weekly academic challenges for all the home teams by scheduling and recording the winning team for each round of the challenge questions events. (See chapter 4.)

WRITTEN COMMENTS

Reading *only* written comments on their assignments and other submitted documents such as quizzes, projects, and the like may come as a shock to some students. Depending on when Forgiving Learning is initiated in the classroom, students could have had up to twelve years of receiving only grades and/or scores on their submissions to their teachers. They may be under the impression that it is the only acceptable way of communicating to students about the quality of their work. (See chapter 1.)

EVALUATE

Using comments to evaluate their academic strengths, weaknesses, and directions on how to improve their learning are keys to any coaching endeavor. This is what good coaches do in the athletic arena and academic coaches should teach and evaluate similarly in the classroom arena.

Students will want to know what a teacher's written comments really *mean*. Writing these comments creates a record of teacher evaluations of a student's progress or lack thereof.

PROFESSIONAL OPINION

What many students may want to know is how a comment like "You did a great job on this report, Sandra" translates into their grade. It doesn't. It is nothing more than the teacher's professional opinion of the quality of what Sandra had done. Her assignment is now kept in a portfolio with all of her other assignments. That assignment, along with others, is a requirement for participation in the mastery conference (see below). If something needed to be corrected or redone, the coach would have so indicated.

MORE TIME

Written comments take more time than just writing a grade or a number at the top of a paper. Beginning each remark with the student's name makes the comment personal, just as one would if talking to them verbally. "Alicia, you began well with the data, but got confused when graphing it. Try again and see me for help if needed." From a very young age most students have been well versed in written communication via e-mail, texting, and the like.

RESPONSIBILITIES

Written comments on social media are ubiquitous. "Talking" to one's students through the comment makes its message more meaningful. Teachers have only a limited amount of time each day that is focused on their work with students. Not only is he/she a teacher but, more than likely, he/she also has family and other responsibilities.

FEWER ASSIGNMENTS

To address this very practical issue it is suggested that fewer assignments be given so as to make the very valuable teacher response on each more doable. Students should have feedback on each submitted assignment as soon as possible. Fewer assignments that go deeper into the content is more satisfying for the student. Student comprehension and digestion of course/grade-level content is improved with a greater concentration on the key elements of the curriculum rather than attempting to cover large swathes of concepts just to meet pacing protocol, especially when it is externally mandated.

MISTAKES FORGIVEN WHEN READDRESSED

The central theme of Forgiving Learning is that students will have the opportunity to revisit their mistakes over and over until satisfactory comprehension is achieved. We can all learn from our mistakes. It is the natural way in which we humans make progress. Forgiving Learning systematizes what is part of the human condition into the artificial structure of classroom. It gives the students hope that their errors are redeemable. From a baby learning to walk to a teenager learning to shoot a basketball, mistakes will be made. Whether they forgive themselves for the missed shot or just continue to persist in trying to walk, the result is a continuation of the activity until satisfied with the results. (See chapter 1).

PERSISTENCE

Parents, teachers, and other adults who nurture learners along in these and other similar endeavors should come to it with a belief that persistence is to be valued above "closure." In the ordinary classroom there is often a rush to have students complete assignments and assessments in a set amount of time. Then, when that time period is over, all is submitted to the instructor for evaluation.

CLOSURE

When the grade or score is given and recorded the whole process is brought to an end: "closure." Forgiving Learning keeps the process open for repeated attempts by the student to rectify what was lacking to the satisfaction of the teacher, *all without penalty*. This is no different than what an athletic coach or a director of a movie requires of the participants: to revisit the play or scene over and over until it is done to the satisfaction of the "coach."

PORTFOLIO OF WORK

All student written assignments and assessments are to be kept in either paper or electronic formats. All of the student work should have already been evaluated by the instructor and contain summary comments written to the student. This not only respects all that the student has done, but also provides for multiple sources of evidence to be reviewed during student-teacher conferences to assess progress. Following the mastery conference (below), these portfolios will be reviewed and signed by a parent/guardian and returned to the instructor. (See chapter 1.)

VERIFICATION

This student portfolio is also critical for review by parents and administrators as concrete verification of the basis for summative student evaluations at the end of grading periods. Some schools and districts may have developed more holistic forms of reporting on student progress than the traditional "grades" on a report card. In either situation the professional in the classroom must call on both what is contained within the portfolio as well as the teacher's experience of each student's desire to learn within their physical and mental limitations.

CHALLENGE QUESTIONS

During the mastery conferences described below students will be demonstrating their understanding by explaining their answers to verbal questions posed by the coach. For many students, defending their answers may not be part of the "normal" classroom assessments. To do this takes both modeling and practice. The weekly challenge questions provide an opportunity to do both. (See chapter 4.)

ARTICULATION

Preparation for standardized state and district testing has so infiltrated our schools that teachers are often forced to use the same multiple choice/ short answer formats for ordinary classroom formative and summative assessments. In responding to the challenge questions students learn to articulate their responses. This not only builds their language skills, but also improves their communication with others on the team.

GUESSING

Very often, assessments of student comprehension just focus on the "correct answer" rather than evidence that the student has a cogent justification for the answer. It is very possible that students can select the correct answer for the wrong reasons or worse just guess with a hope that they get it correct. Guessing is often encouraged with strategies to arrive at what is hoped to be the right answer. This promotes dishonesty. Rather than just admitting that they do not have confidence that they know the right answer, they attempt to trick the test maker/scorer into thinking otherwise. The message the student gets is that getting a higher score is what is valued, not facing the truth that one does not grasp the concepts the question is addressing.

MASTERY CONFERENCE

Mastery conferences can be done either with individual students or with a team of students. The conferences are held every three to six weeks depending on the length and content of the unit of study. Prior to the conference students have already had the opportunity to practice their responses during the challenge questions. They know what the key concepts are and what level of comprehension their coach is expecting of them. Depending on the content, it is suggested that no more than two or three questions be asked. These should be the fundamental queries that capture the core concepts of the unit. When mastering as a team, the coach would ask the whole team such a question and give them a few minutes to discuss and think about it. (See chapter 1.)

SELECT ONE

The instructor would then return and select one of the students to answer. Following that answer, then ask the others in turn whether or not they agree or want to add or delete from that answer. How does the coach know if the student who answers really understands the answer just given or is parroting back what he/she heard in the discussion? The answer is simple. Ask that student to justify what was said and explain it in another way. Using this approach it will soon become evident what the student understands.

RETURN

Based on their responses to the two to three separate questions the coach has asked during the master conference class period, the team will have either mastered all the questions by giving answers the coach considers satisfactory or they will need to return as a team (or individually) to be given a nuanced form of the question(s) that they couldn't answer well enough before and give it another try to achieve mastery. Thus the mastery conference is not just an assessment but also a learning experience.

RECORD AN M

During the mastery conference care is taken to make sure they comprehend the question. Then their answers are fed back to them in order to validate that what they have said is understood. If they answer all of the questions correctly then they have mastered that unit and an "M" is recorded in the grade book/program. For those who do not master they are to write the question(s) they did not explain correctly on a mastery conference sheet. This mastery conference sheet becomes a cover sheet stapled to all the assignments for that unit.

RETURNING

These assignments have all been read by their coach and signed by a parent/guardian. They can return *as many times as they would like* to complete their mastery until the beginning of the mastery conference of the next unit. The vast majority of students usually have one or two questions to master. We usually meet before or after school, on a break or at lunch to complete their mastery.

NOT IN THE GARBAGE CAN

So no longer is the "test" over and done with and thrown in the garbage can, purged from the students' short-term memory. The opportunity to continue to return *is* the soil for learning. There has been nothing as satisfying as the looks on students' faces when they finally master. The sense of fulfillment and internal ascent "that they really do understand it now" is evident in our conversations and discussions with their fellow students.

SURVEY

A survey was taken of the physics students to find out if they would be just as satisfied with being able to retake a written exam over and over until mastered. To a person they said "it just wouldn't be the same." When questioned further it came down to the satisfaction of the interactions with their coach. A positive facial expression coupled with their internal awareness that their coach knows without a doubt that "they have really mastered this" is a real confidence builder for them. They can be successful.

GRADES ARE PROBLEMATIC

Attempting to summarize a student's strengths, weaknesses, and paths to improvement into a solitary symbol is not only impossible but it is also an affront to the dignity and respect that is due to each student. It is fallacious to think that the complex issues surrounding student learning can be homogenized into a lone mark. Complex entities deserve a complex evaluation. The attempt to reify (make into a concrete entity) a multifaceted process such as student learning into a concrete singularity is invalid. Students deserve more than that. In the real world someone who is responsible for evaluating another does so with respect. They meet with that person, discuss the assessor's observations, and come to some type of conclusion with them that is consistent with the guidelines of the enterprise.

ASSIGNMENT OF GRADES

Whether it is within the context of a business, military, religious organization, or some other human enterprise, personal dignity and due process are central to a just evaluation. Imagine going to a doctor for a physical that follows a whole set of medical tests only to have the doctor enter the examination room, say, "C–" and walk out. Wouldn't this be considered unprofessional and a personal insult? But this is often what happens to students when they see their grade posted or see it just appear on their report card. Likewise, a student deserves to participate in a cogent discussion of his/her progress and have input into the assignment of a grade. How this input happens is determined by the coach. (See chapter 1.)

MASTERY IS THE KEY

In chapter 1 grades were discussed as being one of the four basic fears a student has when entering the classroom. This grade anxiety also contributes to the downshifting of the brain's neocortex to the fight or flight functioning of the reptilian brain. One way to minimize the fear is to give the student *some* control over their grades. This has to be done in such a way that respects the instructor's role as a professional evaluator of student progress, and at the same time including the student's self-analysis of his/her progress.

CONTROL

The student-teacher mastery conference can set forth the conditions for some student control. Because *all* the assignments must be done to the coach's satisfaction (even with errors being forgiven and redone properly) before the mastery conferences can take place, the coach can set up a structure like the one below to give the students guidelines on the type of grades that are possible. Students having a real say in their grade is both respectful and just.

SUGGESTED GRADE GUIDELINES

It is all a matter of student control with teacher-developed conditions for grade assignments based on the suggested grade principles below. The highest grade a student can assign themselves on the report card is as follows:

"A" This indicates mastery of all the units covered in the grading period. The coach cannot lower the grade.

"B" Indicates mastery of one less than the total number of units covered in the grading period, with good progress on the non-mastered unit(s). The coach cannot lower but can raise the grade.

"C" Indicates mastery of one less than the total number of units covered in the grading period, with little progress on the remaining unit(s). The coach cannot lower but can raise the grade.

"D" There are no "D" grades assigned. This grade is often considered *passing* in most courses. However, for the purpose of Forgiving Learning, insufficient effort has been made to redo assignments and/or return to complete the mastery conference.

"F" Indicates mastery of none of the units covered in the grading period, with little or no progress on each of the others.

LESSONS OF THE KARATE KID

The whole point of telling the story of the Karate Kid is to provide good reasoning for students to be patient with whatever is assigned by the coach. Although the reasons behind an activity or rationale may not be obvious at the outset, it will become clear and its context will be explained when appropriate. The message to the student is to trust the coach that he/she is a professional who knows what he/she is doing and will explain its meaningfulness in due time. (See chapter 3.)

STEREOTYPES

Developing camaraderie on a team is a challenge. Stereotyping can become a block to developing healthy relationships among students. Intrateam communication is enhanced when no one is excluded because of prejudice and/or negative judgments of others. (See chapter 3.)

NEGATIVE CRITICISM

There is an old saying that says, "Sticks and stones can break my bones, but words will never hurt me." While this may seem like a way to protect oneself from the harsh and derogatory comments of others, in reality the misspoken words of some can demean and cause angst in fellow students. This again contributes to downshifting their reptilian brain into a fight or flight mode. The best way to prevent the downshift in a teammate is for students to be aware of the possible consequences of what they say to a fellow team member and to refrain from such comments. Because this is not always possible, the doll exercise described in chapter 3 will hopefully elicit a degree of compassion that students can be aware of as they converse with others. (See chapter 3.)

THOUGHTS VS. FEELINGS

This may be one of those exercises in which the Karate Kid example could apply. Students may want to know why distinguishing between thoughts and feelings and even describing feelings has any place in fifth grade or a calculus class. The answer is simple. Open and honest communication with other students and their instructor is a critical aspect of learning. It enables the old mammalian brain (limbic system) to judge the relational environment as supportive. (See chapter 3.)

SENSITIVITY

This in turn makes the neocortex (where learning takes place) function more effectively. How can a student discuss the geography of Europe or a challenging math problem if he/she is feeling depressed over a family situation? Sensitivity to how a fellow student is feeling invites listening on a deeper level. It can also make students aware of what events are going on in their lives that are impacting their learning.

OPINIONS VS. VALUES

When working with fellow students in the classroom or with others in the outside world, many disagreements occur because of a difference in opinions that flow from conflicting values. Whether arguing over what the best radio station is or how to complete a group task, students have a right to their own views on the enterprise at hand. Learning to listen to fellow students expressing their opinion(s) without critique is important to acceptance without having to agree with their positions. Seeking to understand the reasoning of others enhances the process and enables teams to come to a consensus on group actions much more fluidly. (See chapter 3.)

HEARING VS. LISTENING IN CONVERSATIONS

Hearing means that the sound of a student's voice has entered the ears of another student. Listening means that the interpretation of his/her comments has impacted the listener in some cognitive and emotional way. Responding with questions of interest, seeking some degree of clarification, and even the orientation of the head and body with arms opened or closed are indicators of degrees of toleration, acceptance, or rejection. So both body language and checking for understanding show awareness and attention to another student's expressions. When students practice these skills the productivity of their team will be greatly enhanced. (See chapter 3.)

DEALING WITH MISTAKES

The central theme of Forgiving Learning is the enlightening way of dealing with mistakes in the classroom. The coach should establish a classroom culture enabling students to "learn from their failures." This includes not being stigmatized and also affords the opportunity for students to redeem their academic blunders. How students talk positively and negatively to themselves and others when errors are made gives insight into their attitude about failure. Forgiving oneself and others can become a stepping stone to growth and maturity. (See chapter 3.)

AFFIRMING SELF AND OTHERS

What better way to end this time of establishing the Forgiving Learning paradigm in the classroom than to affirm the positive characteristics that each student and coach possess. This feel-good activity is intended to help gel the class into a cohesive unit that can move off together into the academic year. (See chapter 3.)

MYERS-BRIGGS

Students' understanding of their various learning styles is a wonderful tool for them to have in their schooling and beyond. Appreciating and accepting that fellow students also have unique preferences of decision making can make collaboration and communication with them much more fluid and satisfying. The time and energy spent in discussing the application of preferences within the classroom team structure is well worth the effort. (See chapter 4.)

CLASSROOM MANAGEMENT PLAN

Every course or grade level should have a Classroom Management Plan. This should be written in a format that is understandable to both parents and students. For younger students a simplified version should be written in language that they can comprehend. The Classroom Management Plan provides information about the structure and procedures that guide the classroom pedagogy. It should be personal and yet clear about the instructors underlying educational philosophy and expectations. The example presented here is from a high school physics class:

CLASSROOM MANAGEMENT PLAN EXAMPLE

To Students and Their Parents/Guardians:

Welcome to the entry level Physics course! I have designed the course to challenge and encourage high school students toward the exciting experimentation, discovery, and descriptive language of conceptual physics. My main goal as the course instructor and mentor is to encourage and coach students in their learning experience of physics. I will spend a large amount of time communicating with both parents and students concerning the students' strengths, weaknesses, and how to improve in their physics comprehension. Under the Forgiving Learning philosophy of this physics course students will be encouraged to be persistent in readdressing their errors until completed in a satisfactory manner. This applies not only to assignments but mastery assessments as well. Each student will be expected to give an honest effort to learn and to cooperate with others. Parental support and providing information you deem important about your student will enable us to provide the highest quality of instruction.

Sincerely,

Mr. Rog Lucido (physics coach)

The major topics to be covered in this course are: Mechanics, Sound, Atomic Structure, Heat, Light, Electricity, and Magnetism.

The objectives to be achieved are:

a. Students will achieve mastery of course content.
b. Students will articulate their learning both verbally and in written forms.
c. Students will learn how to effectively communicate and collaborate with others.

Course Work

ASSIGNMENTS are to be submitted when due. If a student's work begins to show a pattern of lateness, incompleteness, or poor quality, then . . .

1. 1. Instructors will first meet with the student to discuss the problem.
2. 2. If improvement is not made, instructors will contact the parents and a Learning Contract will begin.
3. 3. If improvement is still lacking, a conference with the student and parent(s)/guardian(s) will be held.

READING HOMEWORK AND TELS (Text Experience Logs) will usually be assigned on a weekly basis. It is *absolutely essential* that the reading and written homework be done each night for each student to be properly prepared for the next day's classroom activities.

ASSESSMENTS will follow the completion of each physics unit—about every three weeks. Students will be questioned individually or in their Unit Teams for mastery of the concepts involved in that unit. If students do not master the current unit concepts on their first try, they will be able to return for other attempts as often as they would like with no penalty. The time period for completion of mastery of each unit will end before the mastery of the next unit begins.

IMPORTANT: *Students must submit and complete all assignment work on time to earn the opportunity to participate in their mastery conferences. If students forfeit their mastery conference because of incompleteness, they must still submit all of their parent-signed portfolio work at the end of the unit to receive credit for the work done.*

PLAGIARISM WILL NOT BE TOLERATED: Any verified act of copying assignments will be met with parental contact and discussion of possible classroom suspension.

EXCUSED ABSENCES

1. Illness—one class period will usually be given for each class period absent to make up any assignments or conferences. For extended illness, please call for assignment arrangements.
2. Athletics and/or school approved absences—it is the *student's responsibility* to meet with the instructor to determine the appropriate assignments *before* this type of absence occurs. Also, mastery conferences must be arranged *before* these absences or a forfeit of that mastery will result.
3. Students will be given one week (five school days) to clear any absence recorded on the office absence report.

UNEXCUSED ABSENCES

1. Class cuts—Assignments will not be accepted. Missed mastery conferences *cannot* be made up because the student has chosen to forfeit.
2. Suspension—All assignments are due on the day of your return. All missed mastery conferences are to be made up asap.
3. Unexcused Parental Requests (written)—These must be prearranged with the instructor and will be judged on an individual basis.

TARDIES: Tardiness to class due to circumstances beyond the student's control will be considered excused. Otherwise, tardies are unacceptable and the step-wise Behavior Contract will be followed.

Texts and Materials

Students are responsible for covering their textbooks and keeping them in good condition throughout the year. Since texts are on loan, students will be billed a fee for lost or damaged books. Students must also come prepared to class with a three-ring loose leaf binder (with a supply of lined paper and 1/4" x 1/4" graph paper), a no. 2 pencil, pen, metric ruler, protractor, and scientific calculator.

Student Course Evaluations

Evaluations on written assignments will be in the form of written comments to the student. These comments will indicate strengths and weaknesses, as well as what may be needed to improve. Students will staple each unit's accumulation of work and must present this completed portfolio to the instructor for evaluation in order to begin the mastery conference process.

During the mastery conference the student will verbally explain and justify their answers along with any required calculations and/or any figures, equation, and diagrams. Following the mastery conference, these portfolios will be reviewed and signed by a parent/guardian and returned to the instructor. Each mastery question will appear on the portfolio cover sheet.

An "M" will appear before each question the student mastered. When all questions (usually two to four) are mastered then that unit is considered complete and an "M" is recorded in the grade book (or grading program). The instructors will utilize the unit portfolio evaluations, student/teacher evaluation discussions, and the mastery conference(s) to determine progress, quarter, and semester grades.

The student will then submit their grade input and the coach will ratify their course grade for the grading period according to the following:

"A" This indicates mastery of all the units covered in the grading period. The coach cannot lower the grade.

"B" Indicates mastery of one less than the total number of units covered in the grading period, with good progress on the non-mastered unit(s). The coach cannot lower but can raise the grade.

"C" Indicates mastery of one less than the total number of units covered in the grading period, with little progress on the remaining unit(s). The coach cannot lower but can raise the grade.

"D" There are no "D" grades assigned. While this grade is often considered *passing*, for the purpose of Forgiving Learning insufficient effort has been made to redo assignments and/or return to complete the mastery conference.

IMPORTANT: Note that our expectation reflected by the above grading scale is on student mastery at the "A," "B," or "C" grade levels. If at any time a student's progress falls below mastery at the "C" level, the student's parent(s)/guardian(s) and counselor will meet with the student and instructor to discuss whether the student should remain in the course.

Discipline Policy

EXPECTED CLASSROOM BEHAVIOR

- *Be prepared with appropriate books, paper, pencil, etc.*
- *Cooperate with all assigned activities and use classroom time wisely.*
- *Respect other students' right to learn.*
- *Adhere to dress code.*

- *Adhere to all school district policies on sexual harassment, zero tolerance, and attendance.*

UNACCEPTABLE CLASSROOM BEHAVIOR

- Entering class unprepared without appropriate materials
- Eating, drinking, or chewing gum during class.
- Any disruption of classroom activities or learning environment.

CONSTRUCTIVE RESPONSE(S)

- Responses to both acceptable and unacceptable behavior will be personal between instructor and student.
- Instructors will make every effort to comment on a student's behavior in a private manner between themselves and the student.
- When this communication seems ineffective, a behavior contract may be utilized, and the student's parents and counselors will be brought into the situation.
- Commendations will be both verbal and written and follow in a timely manner to the student and parent(s)/guardian(s) as appropriate for the situation. A student's desire not to be in the limelight will be respected.

QUESTIONS, COMMENTS AND/OR CONCERNS?

Feel free to call the main office telephone at xxx-xxxx. You can leave a message, or your call may be put through during the following preparation periods:

Coach Lucido will normally be available during xth and yth periods, during lunch, and after school.

Thank you very much.

I have read all the attached information in the Physics Course Management Plan and do agree to the conditions given.

________________________ ____________________

Student Signature Date

________________________ ____________________

Parent/Guardian Signature Date

____________________ ____________________

Home Telephone Number Work Telephone Number

SIX

Integrating Forgiving Learning with an Individual Educational Philosophy

Most people who, over a period of years, have experienced some form of organized education (public, private, charter, or home schooled) develop opinions about what students, parents, teachers, schools, and learning are all about. These opinions, if carried further, evolve into a philosophy of education. Those of us who are directly involved within a system of schooling as educators have perhaps made this our life's work. Students, parents, and the community at large are recipients of that endeavor.

FOIBLES

The Forgiving Learning pedagogy as described in chapter 1 was introduced to me by my football coach who forgave my past failings as a middle linebacker and asked me to be a starting player in a very important game for our team. He realized that my skill level at that moment in my development was more important than a judgment based on my past foibles on the team. He saw that this middle linebacker had "learned" from errors and misjudgments in conditioning and playing my position during the season and was now a better contributor to the team's success.

BRAIN FRIENDLY

What is recognized now from that incident is that my "learning" was a function of how my brain's neocortex had developed new useful programs from failed ones. That is the natural way human learning evolves. So the fundamental philosophy of Forgiving Learning is based for the most part on creating and maintaining a brain-friendly classroom environment.

The brain-compatible Forgiving Learning philosophy is founded on these beliefs:

1. The classroom, site, and district settings for brain-compatible learning should be as *free from threat* as possible, not simply by good intention but by design.
    a. Reduce any adversarial attitudes toward students.
    b. Eliminate using tests, grades, and scores as threats to improve performance and learning.
    c. Eliminate the use of ridicule or embarrassment in the classroom setting.
    d. Encourage as much student mobility during learning experiences within and outside of the classroom as safety and school regulations allow.
2. Teaching content should be age, culturally, and developmentally relevant to where students are in their lives.
    a. Invite students on a daily basis to find connections between what they learned and the real world.
    b. Invite outside speakers into the classroom to discuss the connection between their learning and the real world.
    c. Leave the classroom to go about the campus or on a field trip to draw relationships between real-world and learned programs.
    d. Encourage student interaction with members of the community that would support their learning.
3. Classroom methodology should be rich in communication:
    a. Students should have timely written feedback on any assignments.
    b. Lecturing/discussions should be altered so that there are frequent (eight-to-ten minute) breaks where students can discuss among themselves what they understand, and to clarify and practice.
    c. Classroom instructors should attempt to take on the mindset of a "coach." Students should experience their coach as not just passionate and knowledgeable about what they are teaching, but more importantly fervent about being experienced as a personal ally on the students' side—forgiving their errors and providing them opportunity after opportunity to redeem their mistakes.

d. Teaming with other students should be central to classroom design. Cooperation not competition among students should be fostered in all group endeavors. It should be strongly emphasized that the appropriate use of language during communication is vital for the learning in the classroom and preparation for life outside of school.

e. Wherever possible have students use their creativity in design. Whether it involves words, drawings, plans, construction, decoration, invention, or aesthetics, it gives a student or small team the opportunity to experience the process of choosing among alternatives (self-imposed risk taking) and making the compromises engineers call tradeoffs. Inherently, design entails problem solving and builds those neocortex programs by which previous knowledge can be transferred to fresh applications. This can automatically be put to practical use and enhance communication as well as basic skills.

4. The mastery approach should be used in all evaluations.

   a. Make 100 percent of the key elements the goal, but leave the time for attainment flexible within the confines of a given time period. (A potential employee is not hired at McDonald's to make a cheeseburger 90 percent correctly!)

   b. Students should have the opportunity to return again and again to satisfactorily complete assignments and demonstrate mastery in assessments, demonstrations, and presentations, etc.

   c. Permit individual performance tasks, demonstrations, and presentations to take the place of ordinary written tests.

   d. Assign letter grades as a result of a teacher/student evaluation conference. It should be based on the quality and quantity of key elements mastered within a grading period.

VALUE STATEMENTS

When teachers enter the classroom they bring along with them their personal educational philosophies. Whether directly involved in the classroom or in a related position as parent, student, administrator, or interested community member, you also carry within you an educational philosophy formed from your life's experiences. This philosophy is that set of value statements that define how you see students, instructors, schools, districts, and states in the learning endeavor.

INVITATION

Sometimes these stakeholders choose to give up and/or modify their beliefs to conform to the educational philosophies of their schools, districts, and/or states. You will begin by first being invited to write your personal educational philosophy. You will then be asked to compare and contrast it with the educational philosophy of Forgiving Learning outlined above. The culmination is to look for areas of both harmony and dissonance. With these insights in mind, you will then be asked to examine the possibilities of acceptance or workable modifications.

BEGINNING TO FIND YOUR EDUCATIONAL PHILOSOPHY

Two methods of discovering key elements of one's educational philosophy are described here. The first is to design an ideal classroom learning environment along with a model teaching milieu. Include all that you would want to see and have happen within the classroom, school, and district spheres. Use the areas a–k below as topic headings with your responses to follow in the form of "*In this area I would like to see . . .*"

a. Coaching in the classroom
b. Teaming in the classroom
c. Classroom discipline
d. Role of parents
e. Assignments
f. Assessments
g. Standardized testing
h. Quantitative evaluations
i. Qualitative evaluations
j. Instructor academic freedom (include pacing and scripting)
k. Teacher/administration relationships

IDENTIFYING EDUCATIONAL BELIEFS AND VALUES

Now following each of your a–k "*In this area I would like to see . . .*" statements complete a sentence similar to "*This tells me that I believe in and value . . .*" For example, using "e. Assignments" as the topic heading, one could write, "*In this area I would like to see* assignments that have personal meaning to my students." *This means that I believe in and value* that students should be assigned exercises/tasks that are relevant to them. The compilation of all of these *"This means that I believe in and value"* statements is your educational philosophy regarding Forgiving Learning.

SECOND METHOD

A second method to identify key elements of one's educational philosophy regarding Forgiving Learning is to read each of the four essays below and respond to the follow-up questions. This method will lead you to discover your beliefs and values in the areas discussed in each essay and how they relate to Forgiving Learning principles.

FIRST ESSAY

Student Learning Can Only be Described, Not Measured[1]

Year after year, Mario takes district, state, and national tests. Each year Mario's individual scores are combined with others in his class, school, district, and state. The scores are sent home to parents, analyzed by teachers, districts, and departments of education. Decisions are made about Mario, his teachers, and his school. Belief in the validity of the scores is so strong that most people uncritically accept their truth.

All high-stakes testing is based on the paradigm that learning can be "measured" by using a device that produces a number. Tests play the role of this measuring device and the resulting numbers are translated into scores. These scores are then compared and contrasted and by selecting arbitrary criteria are used to categorize students, teachers, schools, districts, and states. But what if the paradigm is wrong? What if learning cannot be "measured"?

Under the current line of thinking we have had tests for a long time in our classrooms and schools. Every such test has supported the idea that once Mario's test is scored it can be used as the basis for judgments about his progress and comprehension of the taught concepts. The idea appears to be very simple: ask Mario a set of questions, arrive at a number for each correct answer, add up these numbers, and there is his score. There is a fatal flaw in this line of thought.

The process of adding scores must be based on a simple scientific principle: items can only be added if they have the same units. One apple plus one apple is two apples. We can add one plus one and arrive at two because of the same units: apple. One apple plus one orange has no sum because they are different items. Attempting to collect them into a new entity is contradictory to their essence. The combination of one apple plus one orange does not produce an "apple-orange." In reality this mathematical computation does not produce one or two of anything. In fact this process cannot be done.

In current high-stakes test construction each test question is based on a singular standard. For example, let's say that the standard is: "Students will understand the slope of a line." There are an infinite set of questions that can address this standard, but each question will be different from the others, otherwise they would be identical questions. If the test asks five diverse questions on the slope of a line and Mario gets three of them correct we cannot say that his score on slope of a line is three.

These are five different questions like adding one apple to one orange to one banana. Three correct answers cannot produce a score of three. Each question is really a test unto itself and cannot be combined with others. Each question is unique; it stands alone and cannot be added to another unique question.

Imagine a singular test that has questions from mathematics, English, science, and social studies. It is quite obvious that combining the number correct from these different disciplines provides no clarity as to what this score would mean. What is not so obvious is when the exam is a "math" test with questions on slope added to those on geometry to those on equations, etc. This same concept holds true for tests in any subject with differing standards and an infinite set of questions for each.

The very act of counting the number of Mario's correct responses in the category "questions" can only specify that the number of questions correct is "such and such" and not that this number defines any type of conceptual understanding. We delude ourselves into thinking we have measured learning because we uncritically accept the premise that "learning is measurable." Adding the number of correct responses along with some mathematical formulation cannot produce a score. We have been duped!

Therefore if it is impossible to arrive at a score for Mario and any compilation of questions we call a "test" then what can be done to find out what he really knows? Answering a question with a correct choice does not mean he has correct understanding. Not only can Mario guess, but he can also have wrong reasons for the correct answer. Surely if Mario's score is without merit, combining it with other invalid scores in the classroom, in the school, in the state tells us nothing. Can there be evidence of Mario's learning there? Yes.

The evaluator of the test, usually the teacher, can describe the student's level of understanding by using words to articulate his/her comprehension of each question. Well, can't numerical scores also describe? No. A score is a number . . . is a number . . . is a number. It is not a description. It is the interpretation of the scored number that forms a description in words. I am suggesting that we significantly reduce the number of questions on a test to provide the time for a knowledgeable evaluator or teacher to discuss with each student the justification for his/her answers.

To do this instructors need to be in dialogue with students about their answers and record the justification for their commentary. Describing learning uses words just like an artist uses media of varying colors and types as the means to paint the picture of the learning. "Helen you have great skills in calculating the slope of a line but you are not yet able to explain its meaning."

See the *Learning Record* (http://www.learningrecord.org/compare.html) for one example of such a process. This is where the *Learning Record* shines. Because of its structure, information about student learning, no matter how diverse, is organized in consistent, meaningful sections that can be quickly accessed and understood by readers across all disciplines. Another process for describing learning is introduced in "Forgiving Learning," the last chapter of *Educational Genocide: A Plague on Our Children*:

> If not high-stakes testing, then how else are students, parents, educators, and the outside community to determine what students know and are able to do? What system can be placed within the structure of a classroom, school and district to provide authentic information about what students have learned? This assessment can take place in a mastery conference with the teacher in which the student must demonstrate their understanding in any form of presentation, demonstration, portfolio defense, etc. The key to any assessment is the requirement that the student is to justify their understanding.

What should be the upshot of all of this? Our confidence in high-stakes testing scores should take a significant plunge. We should no longer believe that state and national test scores could measure learning. We may have thought we were measuring learning, but now we know that no measurement has ever taken place. We were performing mathematical manipulations that had no meaning in the real world. We thought we could extend these scores to teacher effectiveness, school and district rankings, and comparisons across the United States and the world. With invalid scores, all of this is nullified. Some schools had created "data" walls but now we know they are bogus: there was really no valid data to display.

And so it is finally over. The tyranny of high-stakes test scores are laid to rest. We cannot accept purported test scores and the impact they have on individual students, teachers, and schools without being grounded in a sound understanding of what they are and what they are not. All are now released from the paradigm that student learning can be measured. We are now free to describe student learning as we have done throughout history, "Mario, your paragraph is clear, concise and shows your mastery of English form and content. A terrific job."

QUESTIONS FROM THIS ESSAY THAT CAN HELP YOU DISCOVER ELEMENTS OF YOUR EDUCATIONAL PHILOSOPHY:

What do I believe about being able to "measure" learning?
What do I believe about being able to "describe" learning?
What do I believe about high-stakes standardized testing being able to tell the truth about what students know and are able to do?
What would be my ideal method(s) to find out what students know and are able to do?

SECOND ESSAY

Ten Things Teachers Need to Reclaim Their Profession[2]

Sports referees make split-second decisions. Judges and doctors do too, sometimes decisions that are life changing. Despite the subjective nature of their judgments, they are given respect and trust because of their training and experience, and we most often accept their decisions as valid. This was once the same type of respect given to our public school teachers, the professionals who work in the classroom. But since the onslaught of state and national high-stakes testing regimes, too many teachers have been relegated to mechanized assembly line workers who have little say about the process but are required to follow the company line.

This is in direct conflict with the national *The InTASC Model Core Teaching Standards* (http://www.ccsso.org/Documents/2013/2013_INTASC_Learning_Progressions_for_Teachers.pdf), which give the teacher responsibility to adjust, modify, and pace the lessons according to the needs of their individual students. In today's classrooms, though, teachers are taken out of the equation, becoming functionaries in a system of rigorous "manufacturing" controls by local, state, and national directives.

High-stakes tests are said by proponents to provide "objective" truth whereas teachers' opinions are classified as subjective and thus believed to be less trustworthy. But test scores aren't really objective. Who writes the test questions on these tests? *People.* Who chooses the test questions, the number of questions, the time allowed, and when the test will be given? *People.* Who chooses the cut scores that decide where proficient or passing is? *People.* Who determines the meaning of these scores? *People.* These are all subjective not objective processes and many of these people are not even educators.

Teachers are trustworthy, trained professionals. Throughout the year they have a long sustained contact with their students. They know their students' strengths and weaknesses. Their judgments are based on multiple sources of information over the entire school year and are more valid than the results of a few hours of annual high-stakes testing. Why else would some states, like California, in their Testing Report to Parents, contain a clear disclaimer on the reporting sheet:

> A note on using this information: A single test can provide only limited information. A student taking this same test more than once might score higher or lower in each tested area in a small range. You should confirm your child's strengths and needs in these topics by reviewing classroom work, standards-based assessments, and your child's progress during the year.

California's Department of Education thus admitted that assessments, assignments, and progress provided by the classroom teacher should be the place to assess the real meaning and accuracy of standardized test results. But it doesn't act like it really believes it because schools and districts are judged almost entirely by standardized test scores. Which is a more valid predictor of student success in college: "objective" SAT and ACT college entrance scores or "subjective" teacher grades? Several studies have found that high school grades more accurately predict academic college achievement than any other factor. But still the standardized test remains dominant in admission's decisions.

In many detailed analyses of international tests such as the PISA and TIMSS, as well as our own national report card, National Assessment of Educational Progress (NAEP), what is clearly evident is that poverty and the gap between the wealthy and the poor are the major contributors to test performance. Our top-performing students far outnumber other nations. They come from schools that have less than 10 percent poverty. When we compare these students to the other participating nations we are among the leaders. No analysis in any of these studies points to poorer teaching in America than elsewhere.

So what are some key elements in teachers regaining the professional respect and trust they deserve? State, district, and site practices and policies should:

1. Allow our teachers to use best practices in lesson design and pedagogy rather than canned programs that require rigorous adherence to step-by-step procedures without flexibility.
2. Permit teachers to adjust and modify their lessons to fit their students' knowledge and skills rather than preparing them for high-stakes testing. Forgo all site and district high-stakes testing that is not required by state or national law. Do away with site and district tests used to prepare for more tests.
3. Test score "data" can only become relevant when interpretation for individual students is corroborated by their teachers—individually or in groups—who have evaluated said students using multiple sources of information. No judgments, placements, or qualifications for individual students should be made solely on the basis of annual high-stakes testing.

4. Abolish all goal setting based on annual high-stakes testing scores. This includes targeting students, teachers, and schools for score improvement. Each should be evaluated using multiple sources of information before making plans for any corrective actions. Teams of educators, parents, psychologists, and community members should be employed in developing helpful strategies.
5. Eliminate both scripted and paced lesson mandates. It is not in standardizing our classrooms that students learn to be creative and innovative—attributes that are highly prized in the world of work. Just as the diversity of plants and animals is the strength of the earth's ecosystem, our "edusystem" should model that diversity in the manner in which teachers provide unique lessons using a variety of methods. Standardized sameness is not conducive to students' learning nor is it an attribute valued in our culture—otherwise we would all be driving only Fords and wearing only Levi jeans.
6. Eliminate all punitive policies that pronounce harsh judgments on students, teachers, schools, and districts based on unchallenged interpretations of student test scores. Teacher evaluations of their students' knowledge and skills should be the hallmark and cornerstone of valid conclusions about what students know and are able to do. Instructors are the professionals in the classroom.
7. Codify regulations against administrative use of direct and/or implied threats of repercussions to those teachers who follow their State Standards for the Teaching Profession rather than curricular and/or pedagogy directives that utilize a script-like pacing without allowing for teacher modification and adjustments to fit the classroom clientele.
8. State and/or National Standards for the Teaching Profession should be the guiding principles for all teacher evaluation protocols used by administrators. Terminate administrative "walkthroughs." A thoughtful classroom administrator visitation that respects the context of the lesson with pre- and post-discussion is vital to proper evaluation. Otherwise, walkthroughs become nothing more than "big brother" in a formal setting, keeping a critical eye rather than a supportive stance.
9. Teachers should have the freedom without fear of recrimination to express their professional opinions inside and outside of school sites regarding school practices and policies. Fellow teachers, parents, and the larger community need to hear from the classroom professionals regarding the educational programs at their schools. This will provide open forums for discussion and the enhancement of the school environment.
10. Develop an enhanced parent-teacher communication protocol complete with translators for English learner parents who are not

themselves fluent in English. Ongoing and frequent parent-teacher communication will improve understanding and appreciation of the role each plays in the education of their students and also foster a greater mutual respect.

It will take a coalition of educators, parents, and community members to take this agenda forward. Seeking changes in existing local, state, and national educational mandates from school boards, legislatures, and Congress should be the focus of our actions. This should be of the highest priority. If we want the best for our students, then we need to provide the best for their teachers. When teachers again have the highest community respect and when classroom autonomy is returned to them, students will then be able to experience the creativity of revived and energized instructors.

Stopping the culture of high-stakes testing will be the key step in initiating this process. How long will it take? That is up to us.

Questions from this essay that can help you discover elements of your educational philosophy:

What is my belief about the credibility of teachers in evaluating students?

What are my beliefs about teachers' academic freedom to design their classroom pedagogy in conformity with state teaching standards?

What are my beliefs about teachers' freedom to publicly express their views on school site, district, state, and national educational policies and practices without recrimination?

What are my beliefs about parent/teacher relationships and their impact on student learning?

What are my beliefs about the use of standardized testing in the evaluation of teachers and students?

THIRD ESSAY

On Peace in Our Schools[3]

Learning is a human endeavor. Life is full of different random events. We respond—sometimes successfully, sometimes not. Fruitful actions become reinforced and failures are noted to be avoided in the future. In short, we learn from both our achievements and our disappointments. School is a place where educators attempt to mimic the real world. They create situations that have academic, athletic, social, artistic, or political "lessons" attached to each. Teachers hope their students see the value in what is created and make the connection to its parallel in their lives. Learning becomes more relevant.

Thus, the educators' world view is critical in preparing these lessons. If they buy into the viewpoint that the world is "dog-eat-dog," where conflict between humans, such as aggressive consumer behavior on "Black Friday," is the norm, then they develop ways to mirror that belief in our schools. The fastest, the strongest, and the smartest become the winners and the remainder become the losers. Some state and national education laws legislate ways to isolate and separate one group from another, whether it's students, teachers, schools, or districts. These laws compare and contrast to satisfy a need to validate a "survival of the fittest" worldview.

The high-stakes testing regime spawned by NCLB provides invalid test scores that are then used to promote an incentive to classify and categorize students, educators, and their learning institutions. This degrades and marginalizes what appears to be the weaker in favor of those deceived into believing they are superior. This establishes criteria for conflict and division, pitting one student and educator against another and one school or district above or below others.

The truth is that this is an artificial structure not based on the reality of the human spirit. One only has to see the ways we reach out to each other in times of need like natural disasters to see the magnanimity of the human heart. We reach out to help those in need. This is when we are at our best in making our world a more peaceful place.

In the plant and animal kingdoms life is not about "survival of the fittest" as common lore would have it, but rather survival of those species better able to sustain the symbiotic relationships with other organisms in the ecosystem. It is more a give and take proposition in which one species seeks out its needs while providing a benefit to others. This process is mutual to the advantage of both.

I am glad "survival of the fittest" is not the paradigm from which I base the most meaningful relationships in my life. I seek out common ground from which deeper understanding and appreciation of likenesses and differences can be cultivated. We humans seek peace in our relationships. One of the main purposes of the United Nations is to foster peace between countries: "to practice tolerance and live together in peace with one another as good neighbors" (from the U.N. Preamble). Here at home from the preamble of our Constitution: "We the People of the United States, in order to form a more perfect Union, establish justice, insure domestic tranquility . . ."

We need peace in our schools—peace between students and teachers, teachers and administrators, and schools and the community. One of the steps toward peace is to eliminate the weapons with which we attack each other. We can go a long way in establishing this peace by eliminating high-stakes testing.

Students and educators come to the common ground of school already altered by the aggressive aspects of our culture. Our schools should be a place in which a redeeming society of peace is fostered. Countries thrive with peace. Families thrive with peace. Schools will thrive with peace. Anxiety will be reduced and productivity will increase. Let the symbiotic relationships between humans without the need for winners and losers become the model for our children and a better world.

Questions from this essay that can help you discover elements of your educational philosophy:

What are my beliefs about the world being "dog-eat-dog"?
What are my beliefs about high-stakes testing being a weapon to separate and divide students, teachers and schools?
What are my beliefs about schools being an instrument of peace?

FOURTH ESSAY

Forgiving Learning: Reform Begins in the Classroom[4]

It seems like education is on a neverending quest to be "reformed." The message continues today: "American students are behind those of many countries. Our dominance of military and economic strength is on the decline. We are losing our competitiveness." The root cause of this supposition is laid at the feet of our schools by the corporate world. With many studies demonstrating that 80 to 90 percent of student achievement is due to factors outside of school, how can we consider changes in our schooling as the solution to our business problems?

If we are to improve student engagement and learning, not for the sake of greater profits but for the sake of our children, we need to start in the classroom. It is here where the rationale should be changed from other-centered to student-centered. Each student comes to us with his/her own unique personal history. But students all share a common humanity and are in possession of a human brain.

This brain is the organ for learning—not their liver or spleen! If we understand how the brain's neocortex works we will have a way of designing the classroom and school learning experiences to be brain friendly. In schools we should not develop a learning system and then expect that all students will find learning accessible. Instead, we should seek the healthiest way to cooperate with brain functioning in learning and the best way to extract information from it.

We know the brain operates at peak efficiency when it is free from threat, when the relational tone in its surroundings is supportive, and when food and shelter are sufficient. The brain is a pattern seeker. It wants to "connect the dots" in any learning experience in or outside of school: "If I do this then the most plausible result will follow." It anticipates the future based on past results. It is continually experimenting, learning from its mistakes, and stores those results in expectation of the next opportunity to try.

I once took my five children to a local lake that had a rocky shoreline. No sooner had they exited the van than they ran to the lake's edge. There was a buoy about thirty yards from shore. For over an hour they picked up various size stones and tried to hit the buoy. They rarely did. But they persisted. When they came in for lunch I told them that I was impressed with their desire to hit the buoy and asked them why they were doing it.

Their answer to a person was, "It was fun!" None offered an "excuse" for missing nor did I suggest any. I told them I would like to join them at the shores edge after lunch and record their hits and misses. They did not want me to do that. They told me it would take all the fun out of it. You see, they had accepted misses as part of their rock throwing process. Every throw had an excuse for missing but none was expected and none was given. They rejoiced whenever they got a hit.

In baseball a good hitter batting .300 gets a hit only 30 percent of the time. When he makes an out excuses could abound: "I was fooled," "I swung too soon," "I swung too late." There is a lot of failure in baseball. Why do they still keep coming up to the plate? Each time at bat the players have another opportunity to have learned from their mistakes and improve. They have accepted failure as part of the batting process. They make the reasons and excuses failure the motivation for progress. It is part of the game, as Michael Jordan explains:

> I've missed more than 9,000 shots in my career. I've lost more than 300 games, and 26 times I've been trusted to take the game winning shot and missed. Throughout my life and career I've failed and failed and failed again. And, that's why I succeed.[5]

This is one of the major problems in our schools. We spend much of our time recording hits and misses and subvert the natural learning process. We do not make processing of mistakes the centerpiece of the experience. One of my sons is a structural engineer. He tells me of the many times he must submit his renderings to his superiors and fellow engineers for review. He says they come back "bleeding red." He must repair his errors and resubmit over and over until they are correct. If not done properly the building could collapse. People's lives are at stake.

The common protocol for the classroom from kindergarten to university is for students to submit their work, where they are "graded" and recorded. Then they go off to the next assignment oftentimes oblivious to what should have been understood, but focusing on the grade or score they received on that assignment or test. And so it goes over and over again, embedding in each student's brain that learning from one's mistakes is not the core value. They learn well that the resulting score on each assignment and the culminating grade is what is really important.

So how can Forgiving Learning become part of the classroom environment? Begin by reducing the number of assignments. This will provide an opportunity for students to resubmit their work and for the instructor to evaluate it so that the final result is an assignment that is completed up to the teacher's standards of performance. Students are to redo their work until it is done satisfactorily without penalty, no matter how many times it is resubmitted—their errors are forgiven. They do not have to worry about being penalized but just focus on mastering the concepts. Use the same process on tests, quizzes, projects, and the like. They are given the opportunity to master the concepts or procedures until they are done properly.

Have you ever attended the rehearsal of a performance or a team installing a new athletic play? Does the "coach" watch them then walk up to each individual with a grade or score and then leave? Or do participants do it over and over until they have mastered the scene or play as the coach tells each one with words what he/she is doing right, what each is doing wrong, and how to improve? They do it over and over without penalty until the coach is satisfied. This encourages persistence—a critical life skill.

Our students need to be given the freedom to learn from their mistakes in the classroom environment. The classroom protocol must have forgiveness of errors with the opportunity to reengage as a fundamental element of its process. Education needs to wake up and teach to the human condition. Our children's lives are at stake.

Questions from this essay that can help you discover elements of your educational philosophy:

- What do you believe about the goal of American education being to prepare our students to be competitive in the corporate global economy?
- What do you believe about the goal of American education being to enable students to prepare for their personal goals, dreams, and aspirations?
- What do you believe about the role that a student's life outside of school has on their learning?
- What do you believe about the effect that the Forgiving Learning pedagogy could have on student learning?

You have now used two methods to explore your educational philosophy in relation to that of Forgiving Learning. Now is the time to assess areas of agreement and those of dissonance. Where can you make the Forgiving Learning philosophy your own? Where can you modify your philosophy to be in some congruence with Forgiving Learning? Where are there irreconcilable differences?

Your answers to these questions will become the framework for continued reflection on your educational philosophy in relation to that of Forgiving Learning and perhaps developing your own pedagogy that best satisfies your view of student learning, teachers, and schools. John Dewey, one of the twentieth century's greatest educational theorists and philosopher, was strongly aware of the disconnect between a student's daily life and school life:

> From the standpoint of the child, the great waste in the school comes from his inability to utilize the experiences he gets outside the school in any complete and free way within the school itself; while, on the other hand , he is unable to apply in daily life what he is learning at school. That is the isolation of the school—its isolation from life.[6]

What could be closer to students' daily lives than the way they think and feel? From an infant each student learns about the world through interactions with people, places, and things. Forgiving Learning brings real-life communication interactions into the classroom and models the way learning should be experienced inside and outside of it. Forgiving Learning can become a path to better educational health and wholeness for our students, parents, teachers, and schools.

NOTES

1. Rog Lucido, "Living In Dialogue," *Education Week,* http://blogs.edweek.org/teachers/living-in-dialogue/2012/02/rog_lucido_we_cannot_measure_s.html (accessed February 2012).
2. Horace Lucido, "Ten Things Teachers Need to Reclaim Their Profession," *Washington Post,* http://www.washingtonpost.com/blogs/answer-sheet/post/ten-things-teachers-need-to-reclaim-their-profession/2011/05/15/AFeo3V8G_blog.html (accessed May 15, 2011).
3. Rog Lucido, "On Peace in Our Schools," *Testing Abuse,* http://testingabuse.blogspot.com/2015/02/on-peace-in-our-schools-by-rog-lucido.html (accessed February 5, 2015).
4. Lucido, Rog, *Education Week.* "Living In Dialogue." http://blogs.edweek.org/teachers/living-in-dialogue/2013/04/rog_lucido_forgiving_learning_.html (accessed 4/2013).
5. "Michael Jordan." BrainyQuote.com. Xplore Inc., 2015. 9 April 2015. http://brainyquote.com/quotes/quotes/m/michaeljor127660.html (accessed 4-9-2015).
6. John Dewey, *The School and Society and the Child and Curriculum* (University of Chicago Press, 1900), 75.

Bibliography

American Association for the Advancement of Science. *Project 2061 Science for all Americans*. Washington, D.C.: American Association for the Advancement of Science, 1989.

Ayers, Rick. "Testing and Competition." *Huffington Post*.http://www.huffingtonpost.com/rick-ayers-/testing-and-competition_b_54216.html. Accessed June 28, 2007.

Brazen Careerist. "Central Valley Marketplace." *Fresno Bee*. Accessed May 11, 2014.

Caine, Renate Nummela, and Geoffrey Caine. *Making Connections: Teaching and the Human Brain*. Nashville, TN: Incentive Publications, 1990.

Conway, Martin A., Gillian Cohen, and Nicola Stanhope. "Why Is It That University Grades Do Not Predict Very-Long-Term Retention?" *Journal of Experimental Psychology* 121 no. 3 (1992): 382–384.

Dewey, John. *The School and Society and the Child and Curriculum*. Chicago: University of Chicago Press, 1900.

Dickerson, Bryan. "This is Only a Test: Are the Stakes Too High for a Flawed System?" *New Times San Luis Obisbo*. August 11, 2005.

do Amaral, Júlio Rocha, and Jorge Martins de Oliveira.*The Three Units of the Human Brain*. http://www.cerebromente.org.br/n05/mente/limbic_i.htm.

Einstein, Albert. *Ideas and Opinions*. New York: Dell, 1981.

Fisher, Marshal. "What's In A Grade." *CSTA Journal* (February 1976): 6–9.

Good, Thomas L. "Teacher Expectations and Student Perceptions: A Decade of Research." *Educational Leadership* (February 1981): 415–421.

Gross, Beatrice, and Ronald Gross. *Radical School Reform*. New York: Simon and Schuster, 1970.

Lucido, Horace. "Ten Things Teachers Need to Reclaim Their Profession." *The Washington Post*. http://www.washingtonpost.com/blogs/answer-sheet/post/ten-things-teachers-need-to-reclaim-their-profession/2011/05/15/AFeo3V8G_blog.htm. Accessed May 15, 2011.

Lucido, Rog. "Forgiving Learning." *Education Week*. http://blogs.edweek.org/teachers/living-in-dialogue/2013/04/rog_lucido_forgiving_learning_.html. Accessed April 2013.

Lucido, Rog. "Living In Dialogue." *Education Week*. http://blogs.edweek.org/teachers/living-in-dialogue/2012/02/rog_lucido_we_cannot_measure_s.html. Accessed February 2012.

Lucido, Rog. "On Peace in Our Schools." *Testing Abuse*. http://testingabuse.blogspot.com/2015/02/on-peace-in-our-schools-by-rog-lucido.html. Accessed February 5, 2015.

"Michael Jordan." BrainyQuote.com. Xplore Inc., 2015. 9 April 2015. http://brainyquote.com/quotes/quotes/m/michaeljor127660.html (accessed 4-9-2015).

Ravitch, Diane. "NCLB: End It, Don't Mend It." *Education Week*. http://blogs.edweek.org/edweek/Bridging-Differences/2011/10/dear_deborah_have_you_been.html. Accessed October 25, 2011.

Rogers, Carl R. *Freedom to Learn*. Columbus, OH: Charles Merrill, 1969.

Shell Live Wire. "Why Use Teams?" http://www.shell-livewire.org/business-library/employing-people/managing-teams/why-use-teams/.

Smithsonian. "Inventors." *Smithsonian*. July 19, 1988.

Simon, Sidney B., and James A. Bellance. *Degrading the Grading Myths: A Primer of Alternatives to Grades and Marks*. Washington, D.C.: Association on Supervision and Curricular Development, 1976.

World Economic Forum. "The Global Competitiveness Report: 2011–2012." *World Economic Forum*. http://www3.weforum.org/docs/WEF_GCR_Report_2011-12.pdf.

About the Author

Horace (Rog) Lucido has taught physics and mathematics for over thirty-eight years in private, charter, and public schools. He graduated from St. Mary's College, Moraga, California, with a B.S. in physics/mathematics and did graduate work in physics at both San Diego State University and the University of California–Berkeley. He is a certified Program Evaluator and Meyers-Briggs Presenter. He was past vice president of the Northern California Section of the American Association of Physics Teachers. He was both a mentor and master teacher for Fresno State University as well as Fresno Pacific University. He helped plan and taught at the Center for Advanced Research and Technology. He authored *Test, Grade and Score: Never More* (1993), *Educational Genocide: A Plague on Our Children* (2010), has had articles published in *The Physics Teacher Magazine,* and was a contributor/consultant to *Conceptual Physics.* He has given numerous workshops on Coaching in the Classroom as well as Forgiving Learning using mastery conferences. He was one of the founding members of Educators and Parents Against Testing Abuse (EP-ATA), the Chavez Education Conference, and is the Central Valley Coordinator of the Assessment Reform Network.